A LETTER TO THE POPE

The Keeper of the Nest

A Letter To The Pope

The Keeper of the Nest

INSPIRED BY TRUE EVENTS

JENNIFER WORTHAM, DR.PH

New Insights Press

Published by New Insights Press, Los Angeles, CA

For permission requests, please email: publisher@newinsightspress.com

First edition printed in the United States of America
ISBN: 978-0-9995801-2-7 (print book)
ISBN: 978-0-9995801-3-4 (eBook)

Library of Congress Control Number: 2018957516
Editing: Rick Benzel
Contributing Editor: Diane Donovan
Cover Design: Kevin Barnard
Book Design: Kevin Barnard and Susan Shankin

DEDICATION

*This book is dedicated to my brothers Patrick & Michael
and all the abused children of the world.
Know that you are loved.*

For Catholics, the Church is the home of our spiritual birth. Like a nest, it is a place that prepares us to enter the world. It lifts our spirit like the wings of a bird to the heavens above and nurtures our soul throughout our life with sanctifying graces and the blessing of eternal salvation.

Like a bird far from the nest so is anyone far from home.
Proverbs 27:8

PRAYER FOR POPE FRANCIS

O God, by Your Divine will, you have chosen to vest our Most Holy Father the sacred power to tend to those who minister to us the means of eternal salvation.

We pray that you continue to provide him with the courage, strength, love, and understanding he needs to fulfill your mission, to illuminate all humanity to your word so that they may open their hearts to the glory of your mercy.

We ask that you provide the decedents of your holy Apostles the wisdom to follow him with unity and dignity, so together they may tend to our spiritual needs and bring the love of your Divine grace to our world.

Through our Lord Jesus Christ, your Son, who lives and reigns with you in the unity of the Holy Spirit, one God, forever and ever.

Amen

Introduction

IN THE FALL OF 1993, my family sadly discovered that our parish priest sexually abused both of my brothers when they were young boys. Learning about my brothers' abuse and the events that followed the reporting of these crimes destroyed my family.

My brothers were deeply traumatized by their experiences, and they have suffered from the effects of their abuse throughout their lives. When we learned of the betrayal of our priest, my mother and I left the Church. My grandparents, who were deeply devout Catholics never forgave themselves for bringing the priest into our home. Unfortunately, child abuse does not end with one generation. My brothers' children have also suffered as they have watched their fathers struggle, leaving a legacy of emotional baggage that will likely haunt our family for generations to come.

According to the World Health Organization, sexual abuse is a serious global health problem that impacts children around the world. Although the Catholic Church is currently under intense scrutiny for how it has handled reports of clergy sexual abuse in the past, this is not just a Catholic issue. The sexual abuse of children occurs in schools, day care centers, and other locations where predators have access to children. Tragically, over a third of all child sexual abuse happens in the child's home.

While the Pennsylvania Grand Jury report was profoundly concerning for Catholics, most of the findings were about old cases, which predated many of the reforms the Church has implemented to protect minors. In my journey, I spoke with several leading experts on clergy sexual abuse, and I visited with Church leaders and the President, and staff of the Pontifical Commission for the Protection of Minors. I was comforted to learn that the Catholic Church has made meaningful progress. They have a legion of dedicated volunteer's, staff and consultants representing all aspects of the problem who are working diligently to ensure the safety of all children and vulnerable adults in their care.

Yet, there is far more work that must be done. Many victims and their families, like mine, are still suffering. To heal, we need greater recognition of the deep spiritual wounds we have experienced and ongoing support from the leadership of the Church, local clergy and the community of the faithful to assist us with spiritual healing and reconciliation.

For those of us who are seeking help for our family members who have been so profoundly traumatized we need access to comprehensive long-term treatment programs and services to help them heal.

I have learned a great deal about faith and forgiveness in the past few years. Faith is the complete trust or confidence in someone or something. Faith is especially powerful when the granting of trust or confidence is unmerited, as may be when someone hurt or disappointed you in the past, but you have decided to give them another chance.

Forgiveness is the intentional and willful process by which one lets go of negative emotions such as anger or resentment against someone who caused them harm. The process of forgiveness may also involve restoring goodwill between the affected parties, and viewing the wrongdoer with understanding and compassion. Ultimately, forgiveness is the gift of releasing the need for vengeance. The acts of both giving and receiving forgiveness are powerful forces that enable one to deepen their relationship with Christ.

In this book, I share my family's journey and my journey of forgiveness of the Catholic Church for what it did to my family. Many people have asked me, "How can you forgive an institution that has harmed your family in such a grievous manner?" The only answer I can give is that I have faith in forgiveness. I believe if we forgive the leaders of the Catholic Church and support them in their efforts to right the wrongs of the past, the grace of our mercy will make the Church the place God intended it to be—a glorious place of light and love in His name.

Prologue

I<small>T WAS A</small> warm summer evening. My brothers Patrick and Michael and I sat around the dining room table with our best manners on display, as we had a guest: Father Howard, our parish priest. My grandparents often hosted the priests and seminarians from our church for dinner, but Father Howard was the head of the parish, so we had to be on our best behavior. Grandpa had barbequed Father's favorites, baby back ribs and corn on the cob, and Grandma made her special potato salad and bacon-cheese biscuits.

At the table, we talked about school and laughed about the sponge fight at the car wash the prior Saturday. It had been the annual fundraiser for the church, and we all volunteered; even Father Howard. The boys washed the cars, and the girls dried them. Father collected the money, while Grandma passed out brownies and lemonade to everyone. When the last car was finished, one of the boys threw a wet sponge at my brother Patrick. He dunked the sponge in the water and threw it back at the boy, and an epic sponge fight ensued. Both of my brothers got soaked. Grandma was highly annoyed because the seats of her beautiful blue Cadillac got all wet when she drove us home. My brothers spent the rest of the afternoon washing, drying, and waxing her car. When they were finished, it looked spanking new. Grandma was pleased and all was well again.

After dinner, my brothers and I did the dishes and cleaned up the kitchen. Grandpa and Father Howard went out to the back porch to relax and enjoy the sunset over the mountains. Grandpa lit his pipe, and Father Howard lit up a cigar. My grandfather was the Parish Council Treasurer, so they talked about the new church building and other parish business. A few minutes later, Grandma closed the patio door, clicking her tongue at the men as smoke began to drift into the kitchen.

After we finished our chores, I watched TV with my brother Patrick while Grandma helped Michael pack for his fishing trip. Michael was so excited about his trip. He loved fishing, as most 10-year-old boys do, and this was his first fishing trip with Father Howard. Michael would be spending the night at the rectory because he and Father needed to leave at 4:00 a.m. to catch the morning fishing boat, scheduled to depart promptly at 5:30 a.m. out of Newport Beach.

Once Michael was all packed and it was time for him and Father to leave, Grandpa opened the garage door and gathered a fishing pole, tackle box, and some bait and loaded it into Father Howard's car. Grandma handed Michael a lunch box filled with lots of goodies. I remember how cute Michael looked in his little fishing cap. Tall for his age, he had a lithe build and a head full of gorgeous blond hair. Everyone especially admired his bright green eyes, so full of life that they sparkled like emeralds.

Michael was very excited about his first overnight fishing adventure with Father. He had been on several half-day fishing trips with Grandpa, but he had never gone on an all-day fishing excursion like the one Father Howard arranged. Patrick had been out with Father a couple of times, but he wasn't invited to join on this trip because Father liked to take just one boy at a time.

On his last trip, Patrick had caught a halibut that weighed nearly 25 lbs. We always ate fish on Fridays, and halibut was Grandma's favorite. She called halibut the 'steak of the sea,' and she had dozens of recipes for how it could be cooked. My favorite was when she coated the fish with macadamia nuts and bread crumbs and baked it in the oven. Michael said he hoped he would be lucky enough to catch a halibut fish even bigger than the one Patrick caught.

I gave Michael a hug, and he got into Father Howard's car. At the last minute, Patrick blurted out, "Watch out for the flying batfish. If you aren't careful, they'll jump out of the water and bite your nose off."

Michael's eyes got big, and he looked as if he had seen a ghost. "I'll be careful," he said, and he closed the car door and Father drove off. Michael sat quietly daydreaming about the trip as Father drove the few short miles to the rectory. Then he thought to ask Father a question. "Father Howard, is it a sin to want to catch a bigger fish than my brother did on his last trip?"

Father Howard patted Michael on the head and smiled. "Did you envy Patrick when he brought the fish home?"

"No, Father, I was happy for Patrick. I knew I would get a turn to go fishing with you when I was old enough," Michael replied.

"Well, it's not a sin unless you are envious. However, it would be a sin if you eat the whole fish by yourself. Do you remember what type of sin that would be called?" asked Father.

Michael thought for a moment. "That would be the sin of gluttony, right, Father?"

"You are right, Michael," said Father. "Do you know the seven sins?"

Michael thought for a moment. "Greed, lust, gluttony, wrath, sloth, envy, and pride."

Father smiled. "Very good, Michael, it seems you have been paying attention in your Bible study classes." Michael was happy he'd impressed Father. Father had told him that If he was a good boy, and he did well in his Bible lessons, he might make him the head altar boy next year.

Father turned on the radio, and Michael went back to daydreaming about his overnight adventure. In addition to the fishing trip, he was looking forward to spending time in the rectory. Father had a real pinball machine that he had purchased in Las Vegas, and lots of games to play, like Monopoly and checkers. I remember my brother Patrick often boasted about how much fun it was having the pinball machine all to himself when he stayed at the rectory. I have to admit that I was a bit envious that my brothers were getting to have sleepovers with Father. It didn't seem fair that girls were not allowed to go on fishing trips.

When they arrived at the rectory, Father told Michael to leave his bag in the entryway and informed him that he would be in his office for a bit: "Michael, I need to make some calls and attend to some Church business. You can play with the games while I work, or you can watch TV, whatever you like."

"Thank you, Father, I think I would like to play some games," Michael said as he made a beeline to the pinball machine. Father smiled as he watched Michael tackle the game with zest.

About 30 minutes later Father came into the living room and asked, "Michael, would you like some ice cream? I have chocolate, your favorite."

"Yes, Father, I would like to have chocolate ice cream." Then he remembered his manners, saying "please, and thank you, Father," as he went back to racking up points on the pinball machine.

Father smiled again. Having been a frequent guest at Michael's home, he knew the boy quite well. "If it is chocolate ice cream you wish, it is chocolate ice cream you shall have." Father topped the bowl of chocolate ice cream with whipped cream, and then he put little chocolate sprinkles and a cherry on top. "Okay, Michael, here you go, just the way you like it," said Father. Father scooped some ice cream into a dish for himself and joined Michael at the table. When they were finished, Father said, "It's time to get ready for bed, Michael. We have to get up very early."

"Okay, Father." Michael picked up Father's bowl and

went to the sink to wash the dishes just like Grandma taught him. Father nodded in approval, then he handed Michael his backpack and told him to go to the bathroom, brush his teeth, and change into his pajamas.

When Michael came out of the bathroom, Father was standing in the hallway just outside the door wearing a shiny red bathrobe. Michael had never seen a robe quite like it; it shimmered in the light. Father put his hand on Michael's shoulder and led him into the master bedroom. It had a huge dresser with a big mirror like the one in Grandma's bedroom. There was a wooden cross that hung above a big bed. The bed had a soft black velvety cover and lots of fluffy pillows.

"It's time to say our prayers," said Father. Michael and Father kneeled at the side of the bed, folding their hands and closing their eyes. Father Howard began, and Michael followed along.

"Our Father who art in heaven, hallowed be thy name, thy kingdom come, thy will be done, on earth as it is in heaven. Give us this day our daily bread. And forgive us our trespasses, as we forgive those who trespass against us. And lead us not into temptation, but deliver us from evil."

Then Michael asked for some special blessings: "God bless Grandma and Grandpa, and Jennifer and Patrick, and Mom, and Jackson. God, please help Jackson to be a good dog, so Grandma doesn't get mad at him," Michael added.

Father smiled again at Michael, then he pulled back the covers and told Michael to get into bed. Michael laid his head on the pillow, and he thought it was the comfiest pillow he ever felt.

Father pulled the covers up under Michael's chin, then he bent down and kissed Michael on the forehead. He lingered, taking a deep breath. The boy's sweet scent filled his nostrils, infusing him with warmth. Then he lightly stroked Michael's hair. "Like spun gold," he whispered softly.

"Good night Father," said Michael as he began to drift to sleep.

Father put his thumb under Michael's chin, and Michael opened his eyes. "You are a good boy," he whispered.

"Yes, Father, I try to be good," Michael said. Father smiled, and Michael watched as he walked to the other side of the bed, wondering what would happen next. Michael had never had a sleepover before, and he had no idea what to expect. Father took his robe off, and it fell to the floor. He pulled the covers back and got into bed with Michael.

Michael returned home with several fish, including a salmon. While it wasn't the largest fish caught during his trip, it was indeed the best fish. We ate broiled salmon and roasted potatoes for dinner. Father Howard joined us, and he reveled us with stories about Michael looking out for the flying batfish during the entire trip. Michael looked perplexed as we all laughed in hysterics, imagining Michael looking in the water for the phantom fish. Patrick finally relented, taking pity on his little brother: "I was just joking, Dude, there is no such thing as a flying bat fish."

Michael realized he had been duped. He grabbed a bread roll from the table and tossed it at Patrick, and we all laughed again as the bread roll hit Patrick squarely on the forehead. Patrick picked up the dinner roll which had landed on the floor and got ready to toss it back at Michael. Grandma clicked her tongue, reminding them that we had a special guest. We finished our dinner, ate cheesecake with strawberries and whipped cream for dessert, and did our kitchen chores before watching our favorite show, "Little House on the Prairie." Then it was time for bed.

Later that night as Michael and Patrick lay quietly in their bunk beds, Patrick asked, "Did you have fun?" Michael didn't answer. A few minutes later, Patrick asked, "Did he take you to the big room?"

"Yes," Michael whispered. Then he turned his face into his pillow and cried himself asleep.

My brothers never spoke to one another of their time with Father Howard. He made them promise to never talk to one another, or anyone, about their private time with him at the rectory. Father Howard told them that being with a priest 'would please God' and he told them that the love of a priest was only for special boys, and that they should not tell anyone because people would be jealous. They obeyed because they feared the repercussions of disappointing God. As the years went by, and they came to understand what had happened to them, they kept their secret out of shame and disgrace.

The rest of Patrick and Michael's story is not unlike thousands of other stories of children who were molested by a priest.

Unfortunately, the molestation of children has been occurring since the dawn of time, scarring them for life. Most victims never speak of their abuse.

In years past, victims of clergy sexual abuse who reported their abuse to Church officials were harassed, shamed, and shunned. We now know that some leaders of the Catholic Church routinely responded by hiding the crimes of those responsible, moving the offending priests to another parish, intimidating victims into silence, and stonewalling legal attempts to punish the perpetrators.

This is the story about what happened to my family, who were all victims of the Church's betrayal. It explains why I left the Church after learning what Father Howard did to my brothers. But it is also a story about the power of forgiveness, the love of my faith, and my hope for the future of my Church.

I am sharing my story because I believe we must speak out for the victims of abuse and take whatever action we have within our power to prevent future abuses. We must pray for our Pope and the cardinals, bishops, priests, nuns, and lay leaders of the Church to work together to do what must be done to make things right.

.

1

No words can describe the stunning beauty and majesty of the Vatican. It is simply that: stunningly beautiful and majestic.

In mid-December of 2016, in the very early hours of the day, the sun broke through the clouds, and the dew glistened off the inlaid stone that surrounds the entrance to Saint Peter's Basilica. Shadows were cast, as the sunbeams met the towering Corinthian façade and the prominent columns that symbolize the stretched arms of the church embracing the world.

Such a day was not unusual, as Pope Francis and those who work at the Vatican have seen many similar days. But on this mid-December morning, the Vatican and the Pope would be made aware of a situation that had become all too familiar; one that lingers over the Catholic Church like the gray skies earlier that morning. It was as though God was reminding the Church and the Pope that there are still many souls and wounds that need healing.

The once-promising blue skies and vibrant sun that started the day gave way to clouds and a downpour. As the cold raindrops hit against the Vatican's windows, church bells rang nine times, a tradition established hundreds of years ago. Priests moved about inside the halls and offices, as did lay people who staffed the palace and Papal offices. It seemed like a routine day.

As with any corporation or business, someone is charged with managing the organization's affairs. In the case of the Vatican, the Prefecture of the Apostolic Household is the one who manages the flow of work and information as it relates to the Pope and the Papal family. The Prefecture is the official charged with oversight of the Papal household, which consists of a section of the Roman Curia, including the Papal Chapel (Cappella Pontificia) and the Papal Family (Familia Pontificia). The Prefecture supervises everything concerning the conduct and service of all clerics and laypersons who make up the Papal Chapel and family. He is at the service of the Supreme Pontiff, both in the Apostolic Palace and when he travels in Rome or in Italy.

On this early morning, as the Prefecture made his way along the wide marble hallways draped in frescoes and tapestries, he greeted everyone with a smile and a nod. As usual, he stopped at his secretary's desk to retrieve his daily schedule, along with any letters and documents that awaited his disposition.

With one hand positioned behind his back and the other securing a cup of coffee, the Prefecture leaned slightly over the pile of papers. The secretary looked up, awaiting any comments, as the Prefecture thumbed through the documents and noticed a lengthy fax in the pile. He turned to the secretary, stroked his chin with his index finger and thumb, and commented, "The pile is bigger than usual." The secretary turned to the Prefecture. "It is because there is a very long fax. It arrived last night from America. It was faxed in both English and Spanish!"

The Prefecture's curiosity was aroused. "Anything urgent?" "No, but it is a rather compelling letter. There is a request for a meeting with His Holiness next week. You may wish to attend to this matter," the secretary remarked as he busily returned to his duties. The Prefecture gathered the letters, his daily schedule, and the fax and placed them in his briefcase. He looked over at the secretary and laughed, "I'll need more coffee if I am to get through all of this," as he held his cup and briefcase in the air.

The secretary nodded. "I will have some sent to your office, your Eminence." The Prefecture made his way down the long hallway, greeting his staff as he entered his office. Bookshelves lined the walls, stuffed with books and stacks of papers. Not an inch was spared. As he sat himself down at his desk, he felt ready for the day.

The Prefecture, as those in his position have done for hundreds of years, started his day by reviewing the correspondence and official documents that had been sent to the attention of the Pope. After placing his coffee cup on a coaster, he scanned the screen of his computer and answered several emails. Then he removed the long fax from the American from the stack of letters and began to read.

The words and the message on the pages of the fax immediately captured his attention. Troubled by what he was reading, he wondered how the tragic story before him impacted the souls and lives of those harmed by another errant priest. Then the Prefecture realized this letter was different than others that had come across his desk: its writer had imparted a message of forgiveness and hope following a tragic story of pain and sorrow. That juxtaposition caused the Prefecture to read the letter once again.

He sat in his leather chair and leaned his head back, deep in thought. He wondered if it could be true and debated the contents of the letter in his mind. Moments later, he looked at the end of the fax and noticed a copy of an email from the Sisters of Mercy. The Prefecture read the email several times and was now convinced that the letter deserved the attention of the Pope.

The Prefecture placed the Spanish version (His Holiness's native language) of the faxed letter from the American in the Papal envelope along with a few other documents that merited the Pope's attention. After attending to other official matters of the day, he rose from his leather chair and made his way to the private entrance of the Pope's office.

The Prefecture knocked on the door, as was his custom; a sign of respect for the Pope's privacy. Pope Francis would take refuge in his intimate, private office early each morning, using this time to enjoy a cup of espresso and a croissant while reading his daily briefings. Such was the case on this day.

The Prefecture entered, bowed his head, and greeted Pope Francis: "Good morning, Your Holiness."

The Pope nodded, smiled, and hoisted his cup of espresso in the air. His inviting eyes welcomed the Prefecture, who approached and placed the stack of letters and the long fax into the Pope's box on the Pope's desk. The Prefecture respectfully stood and presented his thoughts on the day's correspondence. "I have several posts for your Holiness. Among the requests is a most intriguing letter, faxed from America. While it's rather long, I believe it is worthy of your consideration." Pope Francis reached out for the pile of letters and the fax, thanked the Prefecture for his service, and wished him a pleasant morning. Once the Prefecture departed, Pope Francis returned his cup of espresso to the saucer sitting on his desk. He removed the fax from the top of the box and began to read.

December 19, 2016

His Holiness, Pope Francis

Apostolic Palace

00120 Vatican City

Most Holy Father,

Twenty-three years ago, I learned that both of my brothers were molested by our parish priest when they were young boys. This news destroyed my family, breaking the hearts of my grandparents who served the Church faithfully all their lives. My grandmother, a devout Catholic, and I sewed vestments and altar cloths for this priest and cooked his meals three times a week for several years.

My grandfather served as church treasurer and helped this priest build the very church we worshiped in for over a decade. My brothers served as altar boys.

My family did not want to pursue a long and painful legal battle with the Church, so the matter was settled for a meager sum; enough to provide psychological counseling to my brothers for a year. Although they did receive counseling, neither of them ever recovered from the deep wounds that haunt them to this day. My greatest sorrow stems from the loss of faith in the Church that my grandmother experienced after learning of these tragic events. She passed away several years ago, and in her final days with us, she questioned everything she had once believed, wondering how God could let this happen.

As have many others who experienced this deep betrayal, I left the Church.

The Pope lifted his head, feeling a deep sadness at this recounting of yet another story of abuse of two children by a priest. He read on, with various expressions on his face, as the writer told of returning to a Catholic church one day and suddenly hearing a voice speak to her, opening her heart to the Holy Spirit, and forgiveness.

I never lost my faith in God, and my spiritual life evolved through the years. I have visited many churches and studied many faiths over the years and learned a great deal from each. With all my worldly knowledge and experiences, I have come to understand that Christ, above others, provides the world with hope and the promise of Eternal Salvation. I recently came to terms with what happened to my family so many years ago, and I have forgiven those in the Church who were involved in perpetuating and covering up these devastating events.

Last year, I encountered a very difficult and serious matter of my own. It weighed heavily on my soul, and it seemed that there was no correct answer. I had not been to a Catholic church other than for my grandparents' funerals in over 20 years. However, for some reason, I felt drawn to a Catholic church to pray on this matter. I wish to present to you the events of what then transpired.

It was a very hot day in the middle of July 2015. Before getting out of the car, I checked my purse to make sure I had my rosary. I had already checked twice before leaving the house, but just needed that last bit of reassurance. There it was, along with the little pamphlet of Daily Devotions which included the Mysteries, the set of prayers that recall events in the lives of Jesus and Mary.

I got out of the car, walked up the pathway, and found a door at the side of the church. I tested it, and thankfully it was unlocked. I pulled open the door and stepped inside, and the familiar scent of incense greeted me, instantly calming my nerves. I dipped my fingers into the basin of holy water, blessed myself, then glanced about to see if I could find a prayer chapel.

Walking tentatively down the side aisle of the church, I peered around the corner into an alcove and found a beautiful little statue of Mary dressed in blue robes with a rosary of pink crystal beads gracefully draped over her neck. She was sitting on a wooden pedestal, and I noticed that someone had placed roses by her feet. My heart warmed as I fondly recalled my grandmother placing roses by the statue of Mary in our church every Wednesday evening before choir practice.

I knelt before the statue, opened my purse, and withdrew my grandmother's rosary from its little gold box. Baby blue Swarovski crystals sparkled as the light that shone through the windows above reflected against the facets of the precious little beads. I made the sign of the cross, kissed the rosary as I was taught by my grandmother, opened the pamphlet, and began my prayers.

When I was finished saying the rosary, I took a deep breath, sat on the heels of my feet to give my knees a rest, and contemplated my situation. My heart was heavy with the weight of the decision I had to make, as there appeared to be no right answer to the difficult dilemma I faced. I closed my eyes and prayed. "Lord, what shall You have me do?" After a few moments, one word came to me: "Mercy." It was faint, like the softest of whispers, and I thought I had imagined what I heard, so I asked again. "Lord, what shall I do?" Then the words became louder: "Have mercy."

In that moment, I had my answer. I would forgive those who hurt me and would leave the job I loved. I would most likely need to move away from my family to find another job. I would sell my home and start over. I struggled to understand why things had come to this point. It was a loss, but my greatest burden was the feeling that I would be disappointing my family, friends, and coworkers. All these people depended on me, and I felt I was leaving so many things undone. I knew it would be hard, and I dreaded the difficult challenges ahead.

My grandmother always said that when one door closes, God opens another. It doesn't mean the loss will be any less painful, but she believed that faith would enable us to endure the difficult times. She reminded me often of the serenity prayer: "God grant me the courage to change the things I can, the patience to accept the things I cannot change, and the wisdom to know the difference." This was one of those times that the prayer would serve me well. I knew that I could not change the circumstances of my situation and I would have to accept that I had no control and that my life would be changing. I knew it was time to open my heart to something new. I finished my prayer, "Lord, please bring me patience and give me courage to face the challenges ahead." I stood, stretched my back, and went to sit in one of the pews near the front of the church to wait for Mass to begin.

I sat quietly and reflected on my life, and I realized I had so much for which to be grateful. I knew many people who were struggling, who had lost their homes, and others with serious health issues. I felt ashamed for feeling sorry for myself. I swallowed the lump in my throat and released the pain in my heart. Try as I might, I could no longer fight the tears and I began to cry. But these were not tears of sorrow; they were tears of relief. The answer to my question was clear, and I was at peace with my decision. I dried my eyes and looked around the church, for the first time seeing it in all its glory.

There were dozens of stained glass windows that sparkled brilliantly in the mid-afternoon light, bringing the Stations of the Cross to life. To the left of the altar was a lovely organ. I imagined a soft hymn playing in the background, and I smiled as I recalled how much joy I had always experienced singing in the choir. Behind the center of the altar, a majestic relief of Jesus rising to the heavens was hanging on the wall. On the right side of the altar was a beautiful golden Tabernacle. I saw statues of saints, and at one end of the church, three crosses accompanied by two Roman soldiers framed a window that looked out onto the mountains.

There were hundreds of neatly dusted pews, and I was reminded of an occasion when, as a young girl, I was dusting the pews in our church in the mountains. It was a cold winter day, and I had taken a moment to enjoy the warmth of the sun shining through one of the windows. I remembered looking up and noticing the dust floating in the sunlight, bathing the entire church in a glistening golden cloud. I felt as though I was in heaven, and I was mesmerized as the fairy-like glitter landed gently on my palms, then disappeared like magic. The sun moved past the window, and the golden dust vanished as quickly as it had appeared.

A noise in the back of the church startled me out of my reverie. One of the deacons had come to light the candles for Mass. I watched as he went about his duties, memories of times past floating by, reminding me of all the times my brothers and father assisted in the preparation of the Mass. Then I realized that the feeling of warmth that I had in my daydream was still with me. While I had been alone in the church for nearly an hour, I had not felt alone at all. "God, you are here with me now. I feel you with every fiber of my being."

I opened my mind and heart to accept His presence fully, and I experienced a deep sense of peace. It was as though He was holding me in his arms. I then felt the Holy Spirit moving through me, infusing me with a deep sense of joy. I realized how happy I was, and I knew I was home. In that moment, I forgave those in the Church who had failed my family; and I forgave all the people who had ever hurt me. It felt as though I had been reborn. I felt no remorse, no anger, no pain, and no suffering; there was only peace.

A little while later, Mass began. It was a Latin Mass. I had never attended one before, and I had no idea where to begin. A little old lady wearing a white suit with a pink flower on her lapel came to sit next to me. Her hair was covered by a white lace veil, and she pulled out a pearl rosary and began her prayers. When she was finished, she sat back against the pew and opened her Missal. I told her it was my first time in a Latin Mass. She introduced herself. Her name was Mary, my grandmother's name. She showed me where to find the English translation of the Mass, and she led me page by page throughout the entire Mass, as my grandmother would have done had she been with me.

After Mass, I felt a renewed sense of hope. I left the church knowing what I must do, and the next day I met with representatives of my company and settled my claims. Several days later when the matter was settled, I got in my car and realized that I had absolutely nothing to do and nowhere to go. I had no ambitions, no goals, and no desires. I was grateful and felt I had to give thanks for the true blessing I had received — I had been drawn, again, back to the Church.

I knelt once again before the Blessed Virgin and said the Rosary. Then, I asked for guidance. What shall I do now Lord? How shall I serve you? I submitted myself wholly to Him and then had a calling to serve the Church as a Sister.

The next morning, I completed an application to the Sisters of Mercy. Unfortunately, I was past the age of discernment, and it became clear that this was not to be my path. In the year since I gave my heart completely to Christ, I have been in a near-constant state of grace. At times, I feel as though my joy will consume me. My life is so full of blessings, and He has provided me with so many opportunities to serve Him, that I am truly awed and humbled.

I feel my reconciliation with the Church was inspired by you, your Holiness. The deep sense of sorrow and anguish you have expressed at the past transgressions of the Church, and your intention to bring mercy into the world, have touched me deeply. I know by your word that you will hold accountable those in the Church who have done wrong to others; you will continue to lead the Church on a righteous path; and I trust you will take steps to protect those of his people who are most vulnerable and in need of our understanding, forgiveness, love, and support.

The Church is an institution. Institutions are merely a collection of people. All people are sinners, and while the cloth does not protect one from evil, we must recognize that those who wear the cloth are but servants of God, sinners on a path to enlightenment, as are we all. Christ's legacy of forgiveness, peace, hope, and everlasting salvation must endure. If we do not open our hearts and forgive all those who have transgressed against us, we will never experience the joy of grace.

I have committed my life to spreading this message, and to sharing the glory of grace with others. I desire to help those who may question their faith in the hope that they too may understand the mystery. I may never be a nun, but I will serve the Lord as a Sister of His people until the day I die.

I am blessed to have the opportunity to visit Rome for the Christmas holiday, December 28 through December 29, 2016. I wish to thank you in person for the true miracle the Jubilee of Mercy has played in my life. I humbly request an audience with your Holiness during my visit to present you with a gift, and to ask that you bless my rosary, which my grandmother held in her hands as she departed this earth.

Your Humble Servant,

Doctor Jennifer Wortham

Pope Francis placed the pages of the fax on his desk. He rose from his chair and made his way to an open window in his office. The cool air filled his lungs, and as he stood gazing at the gray skies above, just then, a sliver of sunlight shone through the ominous clouds. He took a deep breath, sat again at his desk, and prepared himself for the day ahead. An hour or so later, there was a soft knock at his private entrance. The Prefecture arrived and took a seat in the chair across from the desk. Knowing the routine, the Prefecture opened a small journal and waited for the Pope to speak.

They discussed the Pontiff's schedule and spoke of several pressing matters regarding the Papal Household. When their official business was complete, the Pope picked up the letter from the American and handed it back to the Prefecture. "Please extend an invitation to the Doctor for the General Audience." With an earnest look, the Prefecture sat upright and noted the Pope's wishes in his small leather journal.

"I'll make the arrangements, your Holiness. Will there be anything else?"

"No, thank you. That will be all." The Pope smiled at the Prefecture, a sign of immediate mutual understanding that did not require further discussion. The Prefecture quietly rose from his seat and exited the office.

2

DECEMBER 21, 2016. Jennifer sat comfortably in her home office. The patio doors were open, allowing the Palm Springs desert air to warm her as she worked. Her grandmother's nativity manger occupied the corner of her desk, catching her eye as she responded to a dozen emails she had received. Earlier that morning, she placed the cradle with the baby Jesus into the manger and set the North Star on the top of the little stable. She would be away on Christmas Eve, and she didn't want to miss out on the experience of seeing the beautiful light shining down on the crib.

Christmas was Jennifer's favorite time of the year, as it was then that she felt closest to her grandmother. Jennifer fondly recalled helping to set up the manger with her grandmother every year, from the time she was five until her grandparents had moved back to Florida when she was in her early twenties. Setting up the manger was her fondest childhood memory. Her grandmother always allowed her to place the star upon the stable. Her brother Patrick got to place the angel upon the top of the Christmas tree, as he was the oldest boy.

Then Michael got to plug in the Christmas lights, and they would all drink hot chocolate and eat Christmas cookies and gaze at the beautiful white lights that twinkled like a thousand stars on a winter night.

Jennifer's cell phone rang, her childhood memories faded into the background, and she got back into work mode: "Hello."

"Hi, honey, it's your mother."

Judy's voice surprised Jennifer and brought a smile to her face. "Hi, Mom. How are you?"

"I'm wonderful. I wanted to wish you a happy birthday and see how your plans were coming for your trip?"

As Jennifer turned her eyes to the nativity scene, she replied with joy: "Very well. In fact, Mike called me last night. He's having a great time in Italy, and he's already sent me lots of pictures. I'll forward some to you."

"I can't wait to see them. When do you leave?"

"I fly out from LAX on Christmas Eve, and I arrive in Milan on Christmas day. Mike is going to take the train from Rome and meet me at the airport."

"Are you sure you want to be traveling on Christmas Eve? The airport and traffic and everything will be a nightmare," said Judy.

"I can't get away before then. Things are crazy at work." Just then, Jennifer's computer dinged, alerting her that a new email had arrived. She glanced at her screen to see who sent the message. She blinked several times, hardly believing what she was seeing. She stood up, her excitement almost uncontrollable.

"Hey, Mom, do you mind if I call you back later?"

"Sure, honey, I'll be home all day. Love you."

"I love you too, Mom," Jennifer said as she hung up the phone.

Jennifer placed her hand on her forehead, wondering what the email might say. She had just faxed her letter to the Pope two days ago. Was her vision coming true? She opened the email, barely containing her excitement.

From: Julian Lorenzo

Sent: Wednesday, 21, December 2016, 9:02 am

To: Jennifer Wortham

Subject: Pope's General Audience 28 December 2016

The Vatican

Dear Mrs. Wortham,

In reply to your letter to the Holy Father of 19 December 2016, I wish to let you know that you will be able to attend the General Audience of Wednesday, 28 December 2016.

The audience of that day, except for unforeseen circumstances, will take place in the Paul VI auditorium in the Vatican, at 10:00 am. A brief encounter with His Holiness might be expected at the end of the Audience.

Presenting this letter, you will be able to come to the Bronze Door of the Apostolic Palace to collect the ticket (Reg. N° 74428) either on the afternoon preceding the audience between 3:00 pm and 7:00 pm or on the morning of the audience from 7:00 am to 9:00 am. The tickets will indicate the relevant time, place, and access. The Bronze Door is situated in St. Peter's Square where the right-hand Bernini colonnade begins. In the event of any difficulty, you can call this office.

May the Lord bless you with special graces at the coming new celebration of His Birthday.

Sincerely yours,

The Prefecture of the Apostolic Household

Jennifer took a moment to take in what she had just read. She felt nearly breathless as she reread the email several times to assure herself it was real. Her fax to the Pope had reached him, and it just may be that her vision was becoming a reality. She remembered the moment several months prior when she had the vision, she was standing in front of Pope Francis with a gift and a special message.

Jennifer could not hide her excitement when she called her mother back. "You won't believe it, Mom, but I just received a reply to the letter I wrote to Pope Francis! It invites me to the Pope's General Audience and it says I may expect a brief encounter with him!"

"That's amazing, honey. What a journey you've been on since we had lunch last April!"

"Yes, I can't believe all that has happened. I'll call you tomorrow. And thanks for the lovely birthday card, Mom. It meant a lot."

"You are welcome, honey. Hope you have a great birthday."

3

Jennifer hung up the phone and thought of the day last spring when she and her mother talked about the Church and her new mission. It was a strikingly beautiful spring day. Flowers bloomed in the gardens of the historic Victorian homes that lined quaint streets, and the scent of orange blossoms perfumed the air. Jennifer sat at a window table at Martha Green's The Eating Room, a charming American bistro in her home town of Redlands, California, waiting for her mother to arrive.

A moment later, she noticed her mom approaching the walkway, and she got up and walked to the front door. Jennifer opened it for her mother, and they hugged tightly in the doorway, lingering for a few seconds before taking their seats at the table.

Dorothy, who had been working at the restaurant for several years, approached the two ladies as they settled in their seats. "Judy, so wonderful to see you."

"Hi, Dorothy; it's great to see you, too. Do you remember my daughter, Doctor Wortham?"

Judy's emphasis on 'Doctor' was a little embarrassing for Jennifer, and she blushed. Dorothy replied, "Yes, I do. It's good to see you, Doctor; it's been a while." Jennifer smiled, and they exchanged a few words before Dorothy took their order. "I'll be right back with two iced teas and two tuna salad sandwiches."

Judy smiled and grasped Dorothy's hand, thanking her for such a warm welcome.

Reaching down to the floor, Jennifer lifted a gift bag and handed it to her mom. "I picked this up for you during my recent trip to Vermont."

Judy accepted the gift with a look of surprise. She opened the bag and removed a very heavy square object wrapped in pink tissue paper. She unwrapped it and saw it was a coffee table-sized book entitled The von Trapp Family. "This is gorgeous, what a thoughtful gift," she said, beaming as she began flipping the pages.

Jennifer smiled as the book brought back memories of the lovely trip she and her mother had taken to Vermont several years prior. The von Trapp estate sits on the outskirts of Stowe, Vermont, a stunning New England town that is a favorite destination for antique hunters, ski enthusiasts, and autumn leaves peepers. Jennifer, an avid photographer, visited that region often and loved exploring the narrow country roads and verdant forests filled with sugar maples that surrounded the picturesque town with its quaint shops, famous galleries, and five-star restaurants.

Judy studied each of the pictures in the beautifully illustrated book, running her fingers across the glossy pages as she took in the lovely photographs of one of her childhood heroes.

She loved the story of Maria von Trapp and her family who overcame such hardships and adversity to live the American dream. "When I retire, I hope we can visit Austria together," she said with a hopeful sigh.

Jennifer fondly recalled how, as a child, each Easter Sunday evening, she sat with her mother, curled up on the couch watching The Sound of Music and eating chocolate from her Easter basket. Jennifer dreamt of taking her mother to Austria one day to trace the steps of Maria and the von Trapp children. "I think we should plan that trip after you retire," Jennifer told her mom.

"That sounds like a great idea," Judy said wistfully as she closed the book and rewrapped it in the pink tissue paper and placed it back into the bag.

"Oh, I almost forgot," Jennifer said, reaching into her purse and pulling out a small gold box. "I wanted to give this back to you." She handed it to her mother, who opened the box with excitement. "Grandma's rosary! Thank you for returning it to me. It's very precious; it always reminds me of her."

"Thank you for letting me borrow it these past few months, it was very helpful," Jennifer replied.

Judy opened the box and sat it on the table, and gazed at the rosary for a few moments. It was clear she was lost in her thoughts about her mother. "So, how's Dan?" Jennifer asked, getting back her mother's attention.

"Oh, he's doing very well. I'm really blessed to have such a wonderful man in my life."

"I'm glad he takes such good care of you," Jennifer said.

Dorothy arrived with their order: tuna sandwiches accompanied by fresh berries, artfully plated. "Can I get you, ladies, anything else?"

"Thank you, I think we're good," said Jennifer.

"Okay, I'll be back to freshen up your tea in a few minutes. Bon appétit," Dorothy said with a bit of a French accent before she departed.

"I'm famished," Jennifer said as she picked up her sandwich and quickly took a bite.

Judy watched her daughter and smiled. "I'm so happy to see you eating. I've been worried; you lost a lot of weight these past few months."

"You worry too much, Mom."

"Well, that's my job. You do seem happy; in fact, you're just glowing, so something must be right. A new man in your life, perhaps?"

Jennifer looked at her mom and smiled. "Let's just say I'm happy; happier than I've been in a long time."

"Don't keep me in suspense," Judy said as she nibbled on her fruit.

Jennifer looked out the window, wondering how to share the news with her mother, knowing it might be a bit stressful for her. She took a deep breath. "Well, first, it's not a new man in my life. What I really want to tell you is that I started going to Sacred Heart several months ago. It's a lovely Roman Catholic church near my house in Palm Desert."

Judy looked up from her plate. She raised her eyes in surprise, then she frowned, and a shadow crossed her face. "I don't think I will ever forgive the Church for what happened. I just can't."

Jennifer let a moment pass for her mother to absorb the news, and then she reached out to touch her hand. "I know how you feel. I was angry for a long time, too." Mother and daughter sat quietly, barely eating their food, each lost in their own thoughts. Jennifer broke the silence, a hint of hope in her voice. "I've been very impressed with the new Pope. You know, he apologized publicly for the way the Church handled the sexual abuse cases." She took a sip of her tea, looking to see how her mother would respond to that. Mom remained quiet as Jennifer struggled to find the right words to express her feelings. "I truly believe he will work to make things right in the Church," she said, hoping her mother would understand.

Judy finally looked at her daughter, her eyes reflecting the pain and anger of a mother whose children had been harmed. Jennifer awaited what her mom would say, now wondering how to break the more surprising news to her. She glanced out the window, and then back at her mom as she gathered her courage. She decided to give her the news slowly, first providing some context for what she was about to reveal.

"You know, hitting 50 was a reality check for me. I've been reflecting on my life, I have so much to be grateful for, and I should spend my time doing more meaningful work. I feel it's time to give back," Jennifer said.

Judy's eyes brightened as she gazed at her daughter, who

seemed so young and vibrant to her. "Honey, you have so much life in you, 50 is nothing, wait till you hit 70: that's when things really go to hell in a handbasket."

Jennifer laughed, "Mom, you know you don't look a day over 60."

Judy smiled. "It's the family genes; we can thank your grandmother for that."

Jennifer was relieved to see her mother smiling again. "Yes, can you believe she was playing tennis into her 80s?"

"She was an amazing woman," Judy affirmed as they continued to eat their lunch with thoughts of the woman who had so impacted their lives.

Finally, Jennifer was ready to say more. "I have something else I want to share with you, but I'm not sure how you will take it."

"What is it, honey?" asked Judy, sensing the gravity of her daughter's tone.

"I've been thinking of Grandma these past few months and how hard it was for her when she learned that her cancer was terminal." Jennifer thought of the moment she had to tell her grandmother that the doctors were stopping her radiation treatments because her cancer was too far advanced. "She looked at me with tears in her baby blue eyes and asked, 'What's going to happen to me?' It broke my heart to see her that way."

Tears welled up in Judy's eyes as her daughter talked.

"I tried to reassure her that we would be there for her; that the doctors would make sure she didn't have any pain, and that she would be going to heaven. But nothing I said seemed to work. So, I thought it would help if I could find a priest to visit with her in the hospital, to talk with her to help ease her fears. I left several messages at the rectory, but I couldn't reach anyone."

"I went to the church office and I learned that there was only one priest for the whole hospital. They said it might be a day or two before he could come for a visit." Jennifer paused a moment, then continued. "Later that day, I learned that one of the nuns would be visiting the ward that evening. I asked the nurse to let me know when she arrived so I could talk with her about Grandma."

Just then, Dorothy stopped by the table to clear the dishes and freshen up their drinks. "Can I get you some dessert?"

Grateful for the distraction, Jennifer said, "How about some of your famous carrot cake?" Judy added, "Make that two."

"You got it. Would you care for some coffee as well?" Dorothy asked.

Judy nodded, and Jennifer said, "I'll have some tea please."

"I'll be back in a jiffy." Dorothy said as she departed.

Jennifer continued. "The nun did agree to visit Grandma, but her response wasn't what I was expecting."

"What do you mean, honey?"

"I told her that Grandma had just received the news about her condition, that she had terminal cancer, and that she was afraid. The nun looked at me, and said, 'What do you want me to say to her?' I was really surprised by her question."

Dorothy arrived with their desserts. "Thank you, Dorothy, it looks yummy," Judy said.

"I asked her to talk with Grandma to help ease her fears," Jennifer continued. "The sister did make a visit, but Grandma didn't seem to be consoled. The next day, I walked into her room, and she was crying," Jennifer said, looking off in the distance as she recalled her grandmother's sorrow. "I asked her what was wrong, and she finally broke down and told me she believed that what happened to the boys was her fault. She brought Father Howard into our home, and she couldn't believe what he did. She asked me, 'How could I let this happen?'"

Judy got angry again. "It broke her heart when she found out what happened, and I know she blamed herself. It wasn't her fault. No one knew what was going on. Honey, we were all so, so naïve."

Jennifer nodded her head in agreement. "Grandma wanted so much to help Michael and Patrick find some peace and happiness in their lives. She believed she had failed them, and her imminent death made her realize that she would not have time to make things right. That's why she was so sad. She didn't want my brothers to spend the rest of their lives angry with God and hating the Church. She shared that she was afraid for their souls, that if they continued down the path they were headed, they would end up in purgatory." Jennifer looked down at her plate as she remembered the conversation with her grandmother.

Dorothy came by again to check on the ladies but quickly departed as she realized they were having a private conversation.

Jennifer took a bite of her dessert but pushed it away. She took a deep breath, collecting her thoughts before continuing.

"Grandma asked me to help the boys find a way to make peace with the Church. I promised her that I would. Then I made her the rosary so she would know that I would do as she asked. It was the first time in many years that I had touched a rosary."

Judy took the rosary out of the box and held it in her hands as she looked at her daughter lovingly. "Grandma treasured this rosary. I know it gave her great comfort during her final days with us."

"Thank you, Mom," Jennifer said as her mother placed the rosary back in the box and closed the lid. Judy always knew just the right thing to say to her daughter.

"I remember sitting in church during her funeral, and I prayed and prayed for the courage to forgive the Church; but deep inside, I was still so angry. And since then, I've struggled with how I might fulfill my promise to her."

Judy was surprised that her daughter had carried this burden on her shoulders for so long. "That's understandable, honey. The Church destroyed everything that was good in our family, and nothing was ever the same. We..."

Jennifer interrupted: "I never lost my faith in God, and last summer when I was struggling, I thought of Grandma, and I was drawn to the Catholic Church to pray for guidance. I found Sacred Heart, and right that day, as I sat in the church, I forgave the people who hurt me, and I forgave the Church. It was such an amazing experience. I just let go; I actually felt reborn," Jennifer said, with awe in her voice. "Then, a few days later, I went back to Church to give thanks, and I felt the call to God's service."

Judy sat transfixed, trying to absorb what her daughter was telling her. "What do you mean, you felt the call?"

Jennifer looked out the window again, working up the courage to share her plans. "I know this will come as a bit of a shock to you, but I contacted the Sisters of Mercy to inquire about becoming a nun."

"Really?" A curious look now appeared on Judy's face. It was not at all what Jennifer was expecting, and she nodded, completely surprised about her mother's reaction. "I believe they have a convent here in Redlands," her mother said as though she was talking to herself.

"They do," Jennifer said as she reached for her fork and cut a small piece of carrot cake, and waited for her mother to say more...

"You know, Jennifer, I wanted to be a nun when I was a young girl. I applied to the convent when I finished high school, but the Mother Abbess said I needed to get a college degree before beginning discernment."

"You applied to be a nun?" Jennifer said more loudly then she meant. Then she said in a more reserved tone. "What happened?"

"I enrolled in our local college, and then I discovered boys. I pledged to a sorority and dated the co-captain of the football team, and to be honest, I wasn't the best student. When the boy broke my heart, I left school to go to work in your grandfather's business." Judy reminisced about her life in college as Jennifer sat, stunned to learn this news about her mother's past.

"Then I met your father, and that was that." Judy looked intently at her daughter. "I understand the allure of the religious life. I was very serious about becoming a nun. So, what's your next step?"

Jennifer shrugged her shoulders, then smiled sheepishly. "They actually declined my application. Apparently, I'm too old to be a Sister of Mercy." Judy raised her eyebrows in surprise, and they both started laughing as Jennifer explained, "I got a lovely reply from the Sister who serves as the membership liaison. She referred me to a website where I should go to find an order for 'older' women."

"I can't imagine you in a convent with a bunch of old women. So, what are you going to do?" Judy said as she peered deep into her daughter's eyes.

"I did search the website, and nothing seemed to click." Jennifer sat back in her chair and folded her arms, getting serious again. "I want to focus on working with people who are struggling with their faith, so they may make peace with God and find some happiness in their lives. I am thinking of starting my own order."

Judy sat in silence for a minute, taking in the news. Then in a spunky tone, she replied, "That certainly sounds like my girl; just the way you do things."

Jennifer was pleased that her mother knew her so well that she didn't doubt her resolve to accomplish this feat, just like other goals she had achieved in her life. "I've been making inquiries, but apparently it's a bit more complicated than I thought. It practically takes an act of God. Believe it or not, you need a

Decree from the Pope to start a new order," Jennifer said with exasperation in her voice. "My priest said the first step would be to call the Bishop, but he hasn't returned my calls," she added.

"Something tells me that's not the ending to your story," said Judy. Jennifer looked at her mother, who always encouraged her with whatever she strove to accomplish. "I'm working on Plan B."

"Which is?"

"I don't know quite yet, but I'll let you know once I figure it out," Jennifer answered.

Judy laughed, "I know you will make a great nun." Then she picked up the small gold box sitting on the table and handed it back to her daughter. "Why don't you hold on to this? You'll need it for your next job."

Jennifer laughed. "Thanks, Mom." Jennifer grew quiet for a moment, then continued, "Maybe I'll just write a letter to the Pope."

"Why not?" Judy laughed as she wiped tears from her eyes.

"What are the chances of his replying? Probably one in a million." Jennifer said as she laughed at herself.

"You never know," Judy whispered softly to her daughter.

"Thanks, Mom, for understanding, and for always being there for me."

The phone rang again and startled Jennifer out of her daydreaming. She hadn't gotten any more work done since her mother called. This time, it was her brother Patrick. "Hi, Pat."

"Hi, Sis, Happy Birthday," boomed a deep voice.

"Thank you. How are you?" Jennifer asked as she took a moment to walk outside and enjoy the sunshine.

"I'm okay. I'm on my break," said Patrick. "It's pretty busy, so I don't have long to talk; I just wanted to wish my favorite sister a very happy birthday."

"I'm your only sister," Jennifer laughed.

"Yeah, but that doesn't mean you can't be my favorite sister."

"Good point. Thank you for calling. It means a lot to me."

"Of course; anything for you, Sis. I hope you have a really good day."

They said their goodbyes, and Jennifer finished her work for the day and headed out for some last-minute Christmas shopping. On her way home, Jennifer's phone rang yet again. This time it was her sister-in-law. "Hi, Jean."

A sweet voice said, "Hi, Sis, Happy Hirthday." Jennifer smiled as she heard her nieces begin to sing 'Happy Birthday' in the background. 'Cha, cha, cha,' they said as they finished the song with their little girl giggles.

"Thank you. How are my favorite nieces?"

"We're good, Auntie Jennifer," said Meg, in a more serious voice.

"Are you excited about your trip?" asked Em's.

"I am. But I'm sorry I'm going to miss seeing you on Christmas day," Jennifer said.

"We are going to miss you too," they said in unison.

"I'll bring you lots of souvenirs to make it up to you."

"What's a souvenir," asked Em's, always seeking to learn something new.

"It's a little gift, a memento from a special place far away," Jennifer said.

"Oh. I can't wait," said Em's.

"You girls be good during your break and spend time reading a book every day, okay?"

"Okay, bye, Auntie Jennifer," they said in unison.

"Goodbye, girls."

4

DECEMBER 23, 2016. The night before her departure for Rome, Jennifer paced around her bedroom, searching for the few final items to pack for her trip. Flustered, she stopped to gather her thoughts. Where had her housekeeper put the bag with the gift? Just one more place to look: in the hall closet— and there it was. Relieved, she clutched the bag and made her way to the living room to pack the gift for her trip.

She reached into the bag and brought out a small brown box. She opened it and gently removed a delicate bird's nest. She admired its intricate structure, wondering how such a little creature could construct such a wondrous thing. Hundreds of tiny twigs were lovingly woven together with leaves, bits of paper, and the petals from a bougainvillea plant that crept along her neighbor's wall. A few feathers were tucked into the bottom of the nest, along with a bit of lint the bird must have picked from the exhaust vent of a dryer. There was also a sprinkling of crimson and yellow flowers on top of the nest. It was indeed a masterpiece, as exquisitely beautiful as any statue or painting found in a museum.

She took some white tissue wrapping paper from the bag and tucked it around the nest, then placed it back in the box, taking great care to ensure it would make its journey to Rome in one piece. She placed the box into a backpack that she'd carry on the plane with her for extra safety.

Jennifer then retrieved her briefcase from the closet and began filling it with the items she needed for the trip: passport, a printout of her itinerary, and the small gold box containing her grandmother's rosary. She opened the email from the Vatican and printed the instructions they had sent for her visit with the Pope.

As she prepared for her trip, she thought about her life and the roller coaster she had been on the past 18 months since she had received her calling to serve God. She had met Stephen, a wonderful man, and had unexpectedly fallen in love. She'd put her spiritual calling on hold to pursue a relationship with him, but things had not progressed as she had hoped. She decided to send him an email before leaving for her trip, asking for some clarity about where their relationship was headed.

After sending the email, she shut off her computer and went to bed.

5

IT WAS 7:30 A.M. and Jennifer's cell phone was already ringing. Her heart raced, thinking it might be Stephen. She answered the phone, her voice optimistic, "Hello?"

"Hi, honey, it's your mother."

Jennifer sat up, rubbing the sleep from her eyes. "Oh, hi, Mom. How are you doing?" she said, as she tried to hide the disappointment from her voice.

"I'm wonderful. I wanted to call and wish you a great trip."

"Thanks, Mom, I think it's going to be an extraordinary journey."

"I believe you are right. But, I'm going to miss having you over for Christmas dinner," Judy said.

"I know, Mom, I'm sorry to miss you on Christmas. I'll light a candle for you when I get to the Basilica. We can have dinner when I get back, and I'll fill you in on all my adventures."

"Thank you, dear, I would like that very much. Have a wonderful time. Hugs and kisses."

"Love you, Mom. 'Bye."

An hour or so later, Jennifer did a last check of her list, making sure she hadn't forgotten anything. Exiting her front door, Jennifer pulled her suitcase behind her and quickly walked to her car in the driveway. She hoisted the suitcase into the trunk and placed the backpack on the passenger seat next to her, making sure to secure it with the seatbelt. She started the engine and put her favorite CD, Kenny G's Greatest Holiday Classics, into the CD player.

Driving down the freeway into Los Angeles, her mind drifted to thoughts she had about her visit to the Vatican. She truly admired Pope Francis; she knew how important he was not just to Catholics, but as a spiritual leader to the entire world. On the two-hour drive to LAX, Jennifer thought about all she had read and learned about this amazing man whose gentility and natural charisma had captured the hearts of people around the globe— Christians, Jews, Muslims, Buddhists, and even atheists alike.

He had been elected Pope in 2013, following the resignation of Pope Benedict, by the papal conclave, the meeting of the College of Cardinals who are convened to select the new successor. As Pope, he was the Bishop of Rome, considered by Roman Catholics to be the true apostolic successor of Saint Peter and the earthly head of the Roman Catholic Church.

Previously, he had been Cardinal Bergoglio, changing his name to Francis when he became Pope. He was the first Jesuit, the first man from the Americas, and the first Pope from the southern hemisphere to ever hold this position.

His official title would be His Holiness Francis, Bishop of Rome, Vicar of Jesus Christ, Successor of the Prince of the Apostles, Supreme Pontiff of the Universal Church, Primate of Italy, Archbishop and Metropolitan of the Roman Province, Sovereign of the Vatican City State, Servant of the servants of God.

So much was being asked of Pope Francis, Jennifer realized. The Catholic Church was at a crossroads, with multiple internal problems, while also needing to maintain its moral leadership in the world around many global challenges. The Church had seen a significant decline in attendance in the US over the last 20 years and there was a decline in the number of men entering the priesthood. The Vatican Bank was being scrutinized, many Diocese were experiencing severe financial challenges, some even filing for bankruptcy because of large settlements they had to pay to victims of sexual abuse by priests in their parishes.

The Cardinals had elected Pope Francis to transform the Church and the Vatican and to bring its members closer to the teachings of Christ. He had appeared to genuinely take to heart the words of a fellow cardinal, "Don't forget the poor." In honor of his colleague's advice, he had chosen his name after the renowned St. Francis of Assisi, "the man of poverty, the man of peace, and the man who loves and protects creation," who lived at the end of the 12th century and the beginning of the 13th and had founded the Franciscan order. Following in St. Francis' steps, Pope Francis had proclaimed to all that "We don't have such a good relationship with our world, and this must be corrected."

Pope Francis had broken from many of the traditions followed by his predecessors. He wanted to live as he had as a bishop and cardinal, with a simple lifestyle, exhibiting humility, thoughtfulness, and a focus on social justice. He preferred living in a small apartment within the Vatican complex, rather than in the elegant bishop's palace. He took public transportation and drove his own car whenever possible. As a bishop, he even cooked his own meals. He was committed to helping the common man and the disenfranchised of the world. He sincerely believed that the Church should focus on serving the poor. He had become the "People's Pope," waging war against inequality, calling for social justice, and showing concern about the welfare of those who are most vulnerable and in need of our love and support.

Pope Francis's outlook on his role in the world had garnered him love and respect among billions of people who saw him as a progressive-thinking spiritual leader. He had already made incredible strides to modernize the Church, but it was clear that those changes had not been easy.

Pope Francis had also become well known for his commitment to interfaith dialogue. His own leadership style of humility and respect for every human life has been a beacon for justice and harmony in the world.

Jennifer thought that what had been most unique about this Pope was that he sincerely believed that the world can be a better place. His style makes him accessible to ordinary people of different orientations and beliefs across the globe.

Francis had also amazed many people when he lobbied for the Church to be more open to Catholics who have divorced. He launched reforms to make Catholic marriage annulments more cost-effective and easier to obtain, enabling divorced Catholics to remarry within the Church. He also sent shock waves through the scientific and conservative political communities when he delivered an encyclical on climate change, declaring that Catholic beliefs need to be consistent with evolution and the Big Bang theory. He said, "God created beings and let them develop according to internal laws which He gave everyone, so they would develop; so they would reach maturity."

Jennifer especially admired how Pope Francis was a lifelong learner, focused on becoming a better person through the practice of personal reflection and spiritual formation. In his life, he had shown a great capacity to change. From his humble beginnings as a janitor to his role as a teacher and his rise as a bishop, then a cardinal, he was a reformer and a change agent. The real question would be: how much change could he bring to the Church during his tenure? Would the conservative forces within the Church support his reforms?

Of greatest importance to Jennifer was the Pope's response to the tragic scandals of clergy sexual abuse within the Church. Under his leadership, the Vatican had taken several steps to address the problem, instituting strict policies and procedures regulating the clergy's interaction with minors. He formed a global Commission composed of Church leadership, clergy,

Sisters, and experts on child abuse treatment and prevention to develop initiatives to prevent child abuse, and to help victims heal. He often spoke of the transgressions of the Church and had made numerous public apologies with great humility to victims and their families.

Jennifer forgave the Church, in large part because of the actions Pope Francis had taken. She could not stop thinking about how his leadership could truly make a difference in the lives of Catholics, in world affairs, and in her own life. She had no idea what to expect of her visit. But, she believed it would be a fresh beginning for her family and would help bring closure to a painful part of their lives.

6

ENNIFER ARRIVED AT the airport and parked her car in one of the outlying parking lots, taking a shuttle bus to the terminal. She didn't feel rushed at this point; she had managed to get to the airport surprisingly quickly, without any traffic. When the bus arrived at the Tom Bradly International Terminal, she stood up and got ready to exit, holding firmly onto her precious backpack with the gift for the Pope.

When she exited the bus, the driver helped her pull her suitcase off the luggage rack and onto the sidewalk. When the driver settled back in his seat, he yelled out to her, "Merry Christmas, beautiful lady. God bless you!" The warmth of these encounters vibrated within her heart as Jennifer made her way into the terminal, which was packed with people and luggage in every direction. Long lines dangled from each check-in counter. Carts stacked high with suitcases were being pushed about, their hurried owners trying to make their flights on time. It was Christmas Eve day, and it looked like half of L.A. was traveling to celebrate this special holiday.

Making her way through the aisles of check-in counters, she found the Air Berlin line she needed to join. It was only five customers deep, so she got through the process quickly compared to some of the other airlines with queues of 30 or more people. The Air Berlin customer service man handed her a boarding pass and instructed her to go to Gate 42. The ease of the check-in made it seem that the rest of her pre-flight activities would be a breeze.

Walking towards the security checkpoint at the far end of the terminal, she turned the corner and came to an immediate stop, her eyes widening in shock. There was an endless snake-line of people in the TSA queue. Nothing in life is perfect, just when you think it is. She took in a deep breath, reminding herself to be patient and grateful for what she was about to embark on— the most memorable journey of her life, to meet the Pope.

The line moved painfully slow, but then she heard a group of Christmas carolers singing Silent Night. Their melodious voices lifted her spirits as they wafted up from the lower-level check-in area, rising to the great heights of the international terminal's cathedral-like ceiling. Their sweet harmonies calmed her nerves as her queue inched forward. She was transported by the music to the church services of her childhood, with memories and visions of her grandmother and grandfather, mother, brothers, and stepfather all singing together the same ageless words, 'silent night, holy night.'

The couple in front of her was struggling with their packages, leaving a gap in front of them. She wanted to tell them to move forward, but she could see the man had a baby in a harness strapped to his chest. The baby was crying, and he was rocking it back and forth to calm it down. Some maternal instinct kicked in, and Jennifer tickled the baby's foot. The crying stopped. The baby, with fresh tears in his eyes, stared at Jennifer as he hiccupped. Now that she had the baby's attention, she played peek-a-boo, and within seconds, he became a smiling cherub with a Michelangelo-like face of pure love.

Finally, through the security line, Jennifer reached for her phone, to check the time and review her messages. It was 1:30 p.m. and she had only 30 minutes left until her plane departed. She headed straight for the gate, holding back tears as she boarded the plane. Stephen had just replied to the email she had sent the night before. His answer was clear: he wasn't interested in pursuing a serious relationship. As painful as it was to hear, Jennifer was relieved to know the truth.

7

EARLIER THAT DAY, the staff of the trendy restaurant, The Grille, in Westwood busily prepared for the day. The sounds of pans clanking, kitchen staff chattering, and deliveries being made through the back door of the restaurant filled the tight space as the chef barked out orders, and his staff jumped to attention.

He looked in the direction of one of his best sous-chefs, who was rapidly chopping vegetables, then turned his focus to Gabriel, his pastry chef, who was wearing a white cap and apron embroidered with the restaurant name and its logo. Without removing his eyes from his work, Gabriel artfully topped off little cakes with swirls of icing, giving each one personal attention. Chef watched from a distance and shook his head as he noticed Gabriel's glasses fall down his nose. Gabriel pushed his glasses back to the bridge of his nose and went back to his creation, not once breaking his concentration, even though he felt the stern glare of Chef's piercing blue eyes.

"Gabriel, are you going to finish sometime this year?" Gabriel turned to Chef with a hint of agitation, as there is nothing more irritating to a food artist than to be rushed. "Five minutes, Chef." He wiped his brow and returned his eyes to his creation. He sprinkled the pastries with raw sugar and put two leaves of mint on each one. Then he carefully placed the pastries on a baker's rack. He cleaned his station and walked to the break room to collect his suitcase and backpack from the closet.

Gabriel pulled out a cell phone and opened the Uber app to call for a ride. He headed towards the back door with his bags, draping his apron and hat on the hook in the breakroom. As he left, he grabbed a bag of food from a shelf near the door. He stepped out of the back door into an alley, and within moments, walked to the intersection to meet his ride. As he got there, he saw Joshua and held up the bag of food.

"Hi Gabe; what do you have today for me, my friend?" The fellow smiled as Gabriel described the contents: "Bread, sliced meat, and a few apples."

The man folded his hands in prayer, bowing his head, and accepted the offering from his food angel. "Thank you, thank you, thank you. You are a good man."

A moment later, a Prius arrived at the curb. Gabriel waved to the driver to indicate that he was indeed the passenger. He turned back to Joshua and said, "I've got to run. I'll be away until New Years. There's a rainstorm coming, you know, so why don't you make your way to the shelter in Venice?'

The man smiled as he looked up at Gabriel. "Yeah, yeah, I'll think about it. Have a nice time away." The man waved goodbye as he took a chunk of bread from the bag and began eating.

"Okay. Be well. Ciao."

The Uber drop-off zone was congested with cars full of holiday travelers. Gabe's car came to a stop. He jumped out and grabbed his bags from the trunk. He waved "thank you" to the driver, then he made his way to the busy terminal. Once inside, Gabriel scanned the long lines, checked his watch, and looked at the monitor screen to find his gate and departure time. He impatiently looked again and did his best to assess how long it would take for him to get through the check-in line.

He checked in his large bag, and after clearing security, he stopped at one of the gift shops to grab some magazines, a bag of chips, trail mix, and three bottles of water. A beautiful lady standing in front of him turned back and looked at his stash of goodies. Gabe smiled. "I've got a very long flight ahead of me."

Gabe heard an overhead announcement that his flight was in the final boarding stages. He paid for his things, grabbed his roller bag, and took off on a brisk walk to his gate.

8

THE FLIGHT ATTENDANT welcomed Jennifer warmly as she stepped into the plane. "Happy Christmas, may I help you find your seat?" she asked in a cheerful German accent. The email from Stephen had left Jennifer feeling out of sorts, her smile didn't quite meet her eyes as she said, "Merry Christmas." Jennifer held out her boarding pass, and the attendant pointed her to the right-hand aisle.

She made her way down the aisle and searched for her row. Reaching her seat, she was relieved to see the one next to her was still empty. "Thank you, Lord," she said, and she hoped that it would remain empty for the entire trip. She just didn't feel up to making small talk with anyone.

She gently stored her carry-on backpack in the overhead compartment above and closed the door. She put her briefcase under the seat in front to have easy access to it. She then climbed into her seat and peered out the window, watching the baggage handlers and other airport ground personnel moving about the cargo hold below. Jennifer shut her eyes, emotional exhaustion setting in.

As passengers shuffled past her and settled in their seats, a cheery Christmas spirit was visible on their faces and in their laughter. Jennifer's mind was elsewhere. A flight attendant made an announcement over the intercom: "Happy Christmas. On behalf of the flight crew and attendants, I wish to welcome you aboard. We will be departing in approximately ten minutes. Please let us know if there is anything we can do to make your flight more comfortable."

Breathless, Gabe was greeted by the gate attendant, waving her arms for him to hurry. She closed the door right behind him, and he realized, a bit embarrassed, that he was the last passenger to board. He sheepishly walked down the aisle towards the rear of the aircraft until he found his seat. Opening the bin above him, he saw it was packed with suitcases, jackets, and backpacks. He smiled at the flight attendant, who knew precisely what his dilemma was. She made her way down the aisle, lifting bins all along the way until finding one with space for his carry-on.

Gabe took his seat as a "dinging" sound filled the plane. The flight attendants positioned themselves for the last walk-through and then proceeded with the airline safety procedures. Gabriel wondered why they bothered to tell people how to fasten a seatbelt. After all, how can anyone get to the airport without fastening a seatbelt in the vehicle in which they arrived?

The lights dimmed, and a velvety voice announced what the anxious passengers were waiting for: "Ladies and gentlemen, the captain has indicated that we are ready for takeoff. After we level off, the flight attendants will provide you with a beverage of your choice. Please make sure all devices are in airplane mode. Sit back and enjoy the flight."

Oblivious to what the flight attendant just voiced, Jennifer reached for her phone that was tucked away in her briefcase. She powered it on, brought up Stephen's email, and sent a reply. Jennifer pushed SEND, feeling that she had to have closure on the relationship before beginning her trip. She powered off the phone and put it back, then reached into her briefcase and removed a National Geographic magazine with a picture of Pope Francis on the cover. She opened the magazine to read the article, once again. She loved looking at the photos and reading about his humble leadership and how he was dedicated to helping the world's poor and neglected. He was clearly a different Pope, a "servant leader" trying to steer the Church in a new direction. She felt grateful that she might have a chance to meet this remarkable man.

When she was finished with the magazine, she placed it back into her briefcase, took out the little gold box from inside one of the pockets, and opened it reverently. She removed her grandmother's rosary from the box, kissed the cross, and leaned against the window. Pulling the blanket over her shoulders, she began to say her prayers.

The passengers settled in for the flight, and there was a joyous feeling in the air, as those aboard knew they would soon be with family and friends for the Christmas holiday. The engines revved up to full power, accelerating the aircraft down the runway and thrusting it skyward. Gabriel looked at the gentleman sitting next to him and offered a welcoming smile as he pulled out a book and began reading.

As the plane began its ascent, Jennifer continued her rosary. When she was finished, she leaned her head against the window, thinking of her grandmother, and drifted off to a hazy sleep.

At 10,000 feet, the flight attendants began moving about the cabin. One of them was passing Jennifer's row when she noticed something on the floor. She bent down and picked up a beautiful rosary. She was Catholic, and she admired the delicate crystal beads and the beautiful mother-of-pearl carving of the Blessed Virgin with the solid gold cross dangling in the light. Since it was closest to Jennifer, the flight attendant touched the dozing woman gently on the shoulder.

"Miss, Miss... I'm so sorry to wake you, but I found this on the floor. Is it yours?"

Jennifer was startled when she realized the flight attendant was speaking to her, and as her eyes focused on the rosary dangling in the hand before her, she gratefully replied, "Yes. Thank you. I would have been very upset had I lost it; it is very special to me. It belonged to my grandmother."

The flight attendant admired the beads once again as she held it in her hand. "It's beautiful. Please let me know if there is anything I can do to make you comfortable," she said as she handed it back to Jennifer.

Jennifer took the rosary from the attendant's hand and smiled. "I think I'm good, for now. Thank you." Jennifer held the rosary for a moment, kissed it, and placed it back in the little box inside her briefcase, then returned her head to her pillow. Her mind flashed to the days that her grandmother lay in bed in her home, surrounded by her family, near to death. She was a saint in Jennifer's eyes, as she had lived with Christ in her heart every day of her life.

Jennifer glanced out the window as the plane soared over the mountains east of Los Angeles, heading out towards the southwestern desert and up towards Canada on its route to Germany. There was blue sky as far as one could see. She closed her eyes and fell asleep.

9

A S SHE DRIFTED in and out of sleep, Jennifer thought of the day she sat in Starbucks focused intently on the screen of her laptop, despite the coffee shop's music and the comings and goings of customers around her. Surfing the internet, she came upon the website for the Sisters of Mercy. She read several pages and found an application. She stared at the page for several minutes, hesitating, then clicked it, and an application form appeared on her screen.

The first portion of the form was easy—name, address, age, etc. Jennifer typed the information into the computer. Then the application asked that she attach an essay answering one question: Why do you want to become a Sister of Mercy? She contemplated how she could or should answer. She thought about her childhood, and all she and her family had endured. She reflected on her recent spiritual calling to serve God. She realized the question would require deeper thought and probing exploration than she could do now, in a busy place filled with people. She closed the computer and headed home.

Later that evening, she sat comfortably at the desk in her office, the doors to the patio wide open. The summer warmth of the desert evening refreshed her body and soul. She turned on her computer, and a blank page stared her in the face. How could she express that she simply felt moved by the Holy Spirit to serve God? Her Catholic journey was a complicated one, and she needed the Sisters to understand the gravity of her calling and how much she'd had to overcome to arrive at their doorstep.

She inhaled deeply the fragrant notes of the night-blooming jasmine floating in the air and was soothed by the sounds of the birds singing as the last rays of sunlight draped the mountains. She sat for several minutes contemplating the answer to the question on the application: *Why do you want to become a Sister of Mercy?* Jennifer thought of her childhood, recalling for herself what it was like growing up Catholic.

10

My Catholic Childhood

To say I grew up Catholic would be an understatement because I really grew up in Church. My parents divorced when I was five. My mother and brothers and I moved in with my maternal grandparents following my parent's divorce.

A few weeks after we got settled in our new home, my brothers and I went to our first Mass with my grandparents, who were deeply devout Catholics. I remember feeling such awe, upon looking up at the stained-glass windows with their colorful pictures of angels that glowed with every color in the rainbow and hearing the beautiful organ music for the first time.

When it was time for me to start school, my grandparents enrolled me in Saint John the Baptist Catholic School. Even in the first grade, we began each morning in church, with the Sisters leading us through our morning prayers and the rosary. Then there was a short Mass and a sermon by the Father, who encouraged us to be good and to listen to our teachers. In addition to math, reading, and science, much of the second grade at consisted of preparing for my First Holy Communion.

Communion is the third of seven sacraments endowed to Catholics, followed by the Sacrament of Baptism and the Sacrament of Penance and Reconciliation (also known as Confession). Communion is a key element of the Catholic Mass, during which time bread and wine are consecrated by a priest through a practice called transubstantiation. Once the process is complete, the bread and wine cease to be bread and wine and are metaphorically turned into the Eucharist (the Body and Blood of Christ). Communion is, in effect, the act of receiving the Body and Blood of Jesus Christ into ours.

To prepare for our First Holy Communion, we studied the Bible and learned the prayers we were required to say during Mass. However, prior to making our First Holy Communion, we were required to make our first Confession. Confession is a process during which Catholics obtain absolution from a priest for their sins. Absolution is achieved through sharing our sins with the priest and atoning for them through an act of reconciliation, or penance, such as saying the rosary. The absolution enables us to be reconciled with Christ and the community of the Church.

The Sisters taught us about sin and the process for the confession. I was required to make a mental list of all my wrongdoings, distinguishing between a venial (minor) sin and a mortal (serious) sin. I had to recite the confessional greeting, and then make my confession. It was a bit intimidating, and it required a lot of thought and contemplation. However, the lives of the saints show us that the person who grows in holiness has a stronger sense of sin, sorrow for their sins, and atonement for the wrongs done unto God. The Gospel attests to the importance of this act of contrition and the forgiveness of sin.

I will never forget the day of my first confession. One of my classmates fainted from nerves, and several others reported to the school nurse with stomachaches. I felt sick, too, like I had a thousand butterflies in my stomach, but I knew I had to complete my first confession, or I wouldn't be able to take communion, so I stayed in church and waited my turn, swallowing the bile as it rose from my stomach.

My confession took place in the typical confessional: a two-sided stall with a small door, like a small phone booth, for the confessor and another one for the priest. I opened the door and closed it behind me. The air was thick and smelled a bit like musty socks. I sat in the small chair and put the kneeler down, and it creaked as I knelt on it. A few minutes later, I noticed light coming from a small screen in the priest's stall on the other side of the wall from my stall. This meant that the priest was ready to hear my confession.

My stomach did a few belly flops, and once again I swallowed my fear. I heard a man's voice greet me faintly with the words, "In the name of the Father, and of the Son, and of the Holy Spirit. Amen." I made the sign of the cross and said, "Bless me, Father: this is my first confession, and these are my sins." I began with my mortal sins, then shared my venial sins.

The priest assigned me a penance of 10 rosaries and encouraged me to make an act of contrition by staying the next day in my classroom during recess to help my teacher with whatever task she assigned to me. It was typical that a penance consisted of some type of good deed or act, such as the recitation of prayers—the rosary—or attendance at Mass. Then Father and I recited the words I had been taught by the Sisters: "O my God, I am heartily sorry for having offended you, and I detest all my sins, because I dread the loss of heaven and the pains of hell. But most of all because I have offended you, my God, who are all good and deserving of all my love. I firmly resolve with the help of your grace, to confess my sins, to do penance and to amend my life. Amen." The priest said, "Give thanks to the Lord, for He is good," and I answered, "For His mercy endures forever."

I remained kneeling for a minute, feeling a bit disoriented, the butterflies still kicking around in my stomach, wondering what I should do next. The priest took pity on me and told me to exit the booth and go back to my seat in the church and say my rosary. I quickly got up and departed, forgetting to put the kneeler back up, so I tripped and nearly fell in my hurry to escape the little box.

The Sisters told us that if our confession was true and our intentions were pure, the Lord would grant mercy upon our souls and we would be cleansed of our sins. Catholics are not permitted to enter communion with Christ unless they have been reconciled with him through this act of contrition.

Although Confession was often open to students at school during recess, my grandparents made sure we participated in Confession each Saturday afternoon, so we would be able to partake in communion during Mass on Sunday morning.

Over time, the butterflies in my stomach melted away, and I began to feel a sense of peace when I entered the confessional. The confession lifted the burdens of my sins from my soul and allowed me to be free to enter communion with Christ. There were a lot of things to learn, and it took a great deal of effort, but I was determined to be a good Catholic girl, so I could receive communion and be with Jesus. I said my prayers every night and asked the Blessed Virgin to help me be good.

One's First Holy Communion is a significant event. The child's entire family attends the ceremony, which consists of a Mass and a special blessing of the children by a priest. Then, the families are joined by their friends for a celebration. The celebration is usually a brunch following Mass, with cake and gifts of Holy Cards, and statues of Saints and the Blessed Virgin. Children wear white as a symbol of purity. My grandmother made me a beautiful white dress with lace and silk ribbons. I wore a silver cross, white tights, white patent leather shoes, and a white veil to cover my hair.

I remember how excited I was to take my First Holy Communion. On that day, my grandparents gave me a beautiful little missal to carry during Mass; it had gold embossing on the cover that said, "Remembrance of my First Holy Communion." I was also delighted to discover that my grandmother had placed several holy cards in the front of the missal to help me with my prayers.

My mother attended my First Holy Communion Mass. It was the first time that I recall that she attended Mass with us, and I was so happy that she was with me on my special day. When we arrived at the church, I joined my classmates, and we formed a line that followed Father in the processional. We sat together in the front row of the church, and the Sisters sat one row behind us. Father began the Mass by blessing us with Holy Water. We sang hymns, then there were readings from the Gospel, and then Father's Homily, and then the consecration of the Eucharist, and finally it was time for our First Holy Communion.

As I got up from the pew, I said my act of contrition. I lined up in the middle aisle of the church with my classmates and one by one we approached Father with our hands folded in prayer. When I arrived before him, he held the consecrated wafer in front of me and said, "The Body of Christ." I said "Amen." I opened my mouth, and then he gently placed the wafer on my tongue. I returned to the row of pews, bending my knee before the Tabernacle (the sacred temple that held the Consecrated Body of Christ) and making the sign of the cross before returning to my place in the pew. I knelt and prayed for the Holy Spirit to enter my soul, and I vowed that I would do my best to be worthy of God and to be a good Catholic girl serving others and my community, as I was taught to do by the Sisters.

I watched as each of the parishioners took communion, blessing themselves and kneeling reverently before the Tabernacle as I had been taught. My grandparents took communion, but my mother was not in the line. I looked back to where she was sitting and saw she was gone. After the Mass, I asked my grandmother where my mother was. She told me that my mother had to go to work, but that she saw me take my First Holy Communion and she was very proud of me. Later that same day, my mother returned from work, and she brought me pink carnations, my favorite flower, and she hugged me and said she was proud of me.

Then she took us to Calvary Chapel, a non-denominational Christian Church to listen to the guitar music and attend sunset services. It was a beautiful ending to a perfect day.

A few years after my First Holy Communion, we outgrew our home and moved to Corona. My family could no longer afford private school tuition, so we were enrolled in a public school. The academic rigor and discipline of my Catholic school education had already put me far ahead of my peers, and I felt out of place in my new class. Other kids teased me for being the teacher's pet because I often offered to help the teacher, as I had been taught to do by the nuns.

My grandparents joined a parish called Saint Matthews. We did not have an official church building, so the Mass was held in my school auditorium. My grandfather, who was the finance officer for an electrical contractor, became the parish treasurer. He led the fund-raising campaign, found the land, and helped secure the financing needed to build the church. Each Saturday we participated in car washes and bake sales to raise money for our new building.

My grandfather also joined the Knights of Columbus, and my grandmother worked with the Ladies of the Rosary to decorate the church before every Sunday Mass and on obligatory holidays. She sewed vestments for the priests and made matching altar cloths for each of the liturgical seasons and special celebrations of the Mass. She often worked late into the night, hand-sewing trim on the garments. I loved to embroider, and when I was accomplished enough, she allowed me to help her. My grandmother and I made dinner for the priests a couple of nights a week and delivered the meals to the rectory where they lived.

It was an auspicious day when the construction of the church was completed, and we celebrated our first Mass. The bishop from the Diocese came to bless our church, and he gave us rosaries and held a special Mass. My grandfather served as an usher, welcoming parishioners and visitors to church each week, and my grandmother, who had a lovely voice, sang in the choir.

Our church grew rapidly in membership, and we made lots of new friends. On Sundays, after Mass, we would gather with our friends and go out to breakfast, then back to the rectory to count the charitable offerings. My job was to put the coins into little rolls, which were then placed into a bank deposit bag. Each year, the deposit bag grew bigger and bigger as our parish flourished.

My grandparents were salt-of-the-earth people. They were warm, hospitable, and welcoming to all, and our home became a sort of refuge for the clergy. Every Saturday evening, our friends from church, the priests, and seminarians and occasionally a visiting brother or sister, would come over for dinner. My grandfather would barbeque chicken, hamburgers, and hotdogs. Grandma and I made salads and desserts, and she made a wine-spiced fruit punch which I was not allowed to drink. Long after my brothers and I were sent to bed, we could hear their laughter as they drank the punch, smoked cigars, played cards, and told jokes. To this day, I know of no one who tells a joke better than a priest.

Having such a close relationship to my church and the priests, and those who served the Church seemed normal to me. I understood that these were holy men who exemplified Christ and were sanctified to consecrate the Eucharist. They blessed us, forgave us of our sins, and administered the last rights to those who were dying. But I came to know these men as real people like any of us. They laughed, they cried, and they did many good things, but they also sinned, as all humans do.

Although my grandparents were very involved with the Church, I remember that my mother was often absent from Mass, and she distanced herself from most of our church-related functions and activities. She rarely attended Mass, but she often took us to visit churches of other denominations. She said she wanted to give us "a well-rounded view of God," and that we should experience different ways to worship Christ. Deep in my soul, I knew something was wrong, but I was too young to understand my mother's situation and feelings.

A few years after moving to Corona, my mother remarried. My stepfather was Catholic, but he was also divorced. The Church requires that a divorced person have their prior marriage annulled by a Church tribunal before they can be married again in the Church under the eyes of God. Getting an annulment is an expensive, difficult, lengthy, and invasive process, so many people forgo it altogether. My parents were not interested in getting married in the Church, so they were married by a Protestant minister in the lovely garden of a friend of the family.

My mother was very happy to be a wife again, and my stepfather quickly took on the role of head of the household. They bought a small house, and my brothers and I moved in with them shortly after the wedding. My parents joined a non-denominational Christian church close to our home, while I preferred to attend Catholic services with my grandparents on Sunday mornings. As time went on, I honored my parent's wishes and reluctantly transitioned to their new church.

Several months after their marriage, on a typical Saturday morning, just as we were finishing our chores, Mom asked us all to have a seat at the kitchen table. I thought that whatever it was that she had to talk to us about must be important, as we rarely had family meetings. Dad got right to the point: "I got a new job, and we are going to move to the mountains," he said. Mom obviously saw the shocked expressions on our faces, so she quickly chimed in. "We are moving to Lake Arrowhead," she said. We all looked at her with stunned expressions.

"There's a big lake and lots of things to do. Best of all, we will be close to Santa's Village." Little brother Mike perked up and said, "I love Santa's Village."

"What about school?" I asked.

"Well, Dad is going to move to Lake Arrowhead in a few weeks, and then we will join him at the end of your semester." Always the optimist, I was excited about moving to the mountains. I was not happy at my school, and we lived in a rough neighborhood.

My brother Patrick started to cry. "I don't want to leave my friends," he said. My little brother Mike, still excited about Santa's Village, said, "Maybe they could come and visit us in the mountains." Mom said, "Yes, your friends can come and visit anytime," and then she said, "Of course, you can visit them whenever we come back to see Grandma and Grandpa."

Then it hit me. I'd be moving far away from my Grandma, which would be truly awful. I tried everything I could think of to find a way to stay close to my grandmother, but nothing I said convinced Mom and Dad to leave me behind. So, on moving day, we packed our belongings into a U-Haul truck and drove 150 miles to Lake Arrowhead. I did my best not to cry as I waved bye to my grandmother. Mike held my hand, trying to reassure me. "Don't worry, Jenny, Grandma will come and visit us in the mountains. She promised."

My parents had purchased a rustic little cabin with two bedrooms and one bathroom. While I was blessed to have my own room, I felt guilty because my brothers had to sleep on the sofa in the living room. After work and on the weekends, my father and brothers slowly constructed a new bedroom in the basement so they would have their own place to sleep. Although our home was small, I was happy in our little cabin in the mountains.

My mother worked as a saleswoman in the leather shop in the village. Sometimes her boss would give her the afternoon off and she would take us to play miniature golf and pinball machines in the Arcade.

I was left to babysit while my parents were at work. When my parents were away, my brothers often fought. Sometimes their rage scared me, and I feared they might really harm one another as their brawls would turn the house upside down. They tumbled over the furniture and chased each other around the house pummeling one another. At times, I had to physically separate them, taking a few punches along the way. They both seemed so angry, and I failed to understand at the time why they were so unhappy.

I became a peacemaker and sought ways to keep them entertained and out of trouble. We played hide-and-seek in the meadow near our house with our friends and our dog, Magic. I took them on excursions through the woods, and we gathered pinecones and trapped crawfish in our local creek. We often hiked to the lake, and during the warmer summer days, we spent lazy afternoons swimming and soaking in the sunshine and fresh mountain air. Every now and then their tempers flared, and I had to find a way for them to make up before my parents got home.

We quickly found the mountain community to be a close-knit community. People were friendly, and everyone seemed eager to help one another. I missed my Grandma very much, but Mom kept her promise, and we did get to visit her every few weeks.

A few months after moving to the mountains, my parents surprised us and took us to visit Our Lady of the Lake Catholic

Church, a charming parish surrounded by majestic pines and delicate dogwood trees. We had visited several other churches—Lutheran, Episcopalian, and a non-denominational Christian church—but for some reason, my parents were drawn to this church. We met Father Tulio, and he welcomed us warmly into the Catholic community. He was an old soul who connected with my mother on a deep level. They spent many hours talking, and she seemed at peace with the Catholic Church for the first time. I was so happy, as I loved being Catholic, and I knew my grandmother would be happy too.

Father Tulio talked with my parents and learned that they'd both had prior marriages. My mother had married my birth father in a civil ceremony at a courthouse, and so she was still eligible to marry in the Church. But my stepfather had been married in a Catholic church, and his marriage had yet to be officially annulled. Prior to Vatican II, remarriage would not have been permitted within the Church, but many of the rules and views on divorce and remarriage had changed. Father Tulio worked with my parents to complete the paperwork required by the Church Tribunal, and several months after joining the Church, they were permitted to remarry in the Church.

I loved my new church. I was especially fond of the little gift shop at the entrance because it had beautiful statues of the Saints, and rosaries and holy cards that reminded me so vividly of my grandmother. She had read passages from her missal each morning before starting the day and said prayers and recited the rosary every night before going to sleep. When I lived with her, she often read me Bible stories at bedtime and helped me with my prayers. Occasionally, she would tuck a new holy card under my pillow as a special treat.

Whenever my parents lingered to chat with other parishioners after Mass, I would sneak off to the gift shop to see if any new holy cards had arrived. I would run my fingers over the beautiful cards as if I were touching the ones at that my grandmother kept on her nightstand. Just gazing at the cards reminded me of her, and all the times we sat in church together saying our prayers before Mass.

The altar of our church was framed by a bay of windows that looked out onto a lovely shrine dedicated to Our Lady of Fatima. In the spring, the garden bloomed with yellow buttercups, white tulips, and pink roses. There was a fabulous organ, beautiful stained-glass windows, and statues of the saints that reminded me of my church in Corona.

I recall that one Sunday, the snow began to fall during Father Tulio's Homily. Each snowflake seemed to float for an eternity, creating a soft white blanket around the beautiful Lady in the meadow. The organist was playing a soft hymn, and then the wind picked up, and the snowflakes began waltzing to the music. It was such a wondrous thing. God was everywhere. He surrounded us with his love and awed us with His beautiful creation.

After communion, I was supposed to be saying my prayers, but instead, I was thinking about how much fun my brothers and I were going to have later that day because I knew we would get to go sledding. I also knew we were in for some added chores. We lived on a steep hill and our driveway accumulated piles and piles of snow, which meant there would be lots of shoveling. Mom always made sure we stayed warm and made hot chocolate with lots of marshmallows for us to drink when we came in from our turn with the shovel.

When I turned 13, my parents enrolled me in Catechism

class, as I was nearing the age of Confirmation. According to Catholic doctrine, in the sacrament of Confirmation, the faithful—those choosing to be confirmed—are sealed with the gift of the Holy Spirit and are strengthened in their Christian life. During Confirmation, one makes a conscious decision to be Catholic. The Confirmation is a vow and commitment of one's intention to live a Catholic life.

The day Father Tulio met with me in preparation for my Confirmation, I answered questions about the Catechism and declared my intentions. Then he told me I would need to be baptized and receive my First Holy Communion. I was confused and corrected him: "But Father, I made my First Holy Communion at Saint John the Baptist Church when I was seven years old, and I have taken communion many times." Father looked at me with compassion and said, "You were not baptized in the Catholic Church, and it is required that you receive the Sacrament of Baptism in the Catholic Church before making your First Holy Communion, and both are required before you receive the Sacrament of Confirmation."

I sat there, bewildered. "I don't understand; surely I must have been baptized? I have been attending Catholic services with my grandparents since I was a young girl." Father was obviously uncomfortable with the conversation and did not wish to explain it further. He patted me on the head and told me not to worry; he would take care of everything.

A few weeks later, I finally worked up the nerve to ask my mother about my baptism. We sat in a café in the village, and my mother bought me a hot chocolate with whipped cream and marshmallows, and a sugar cookie, while she drank coffee with cream. I remember she became very quiet, and then she told me the story of my baptism. My heart ached for my beautiful mother who learned that her action of marrying the man she loved would have such dire consequences for her children. I think back on that day and the images that filled my mind as she recounted what happened when I was a baby.

"It started out as a beautiful day a few weeks after you were born," she said. "I had to meet with the priest to arrange for your baptism, and your grandmother had to work, so I took you with me to meet the priest at the church. It was your first trip out of the house since I brought you home from the hospital. Your grandfather bought a little pink car seat and installed it in the passenger's side of the car. I strapped you into the car seat and drove to the church, which was just a few miles from our house. The radio played, and I sang to you while I drove along Ocean Boulevard."

I imagined my mother singing along with a happy tune on the radio, her delicate, melting voice soothing me as I slept peacefully in the car seat. Palm trees were swaying gently in the ocean breeze as she drove down the scenic boulevard that bordered the beach. A few raindrops hit the windshield, and she noticed clouds clinging to the sea on the horizon, which meant a chance of rain. She didn't mind at all; she had come to love the azure blue sea, the white sand beaches, and warm breezes of this tropical paradise. She had grown up in the Midwest with fierce storms and endless winters, and to her, Florida was like being in paradise. She drove along the coast, enjoying the beautiful scenery as though she had not a care in the world.

She pulled into the church parking lot just as the church bells rang. Realizing she was late, she quickly exited the car and went around to the passenger side, opened the door, and gently lifted me from the car seat. The groundskeeper nodded as she quickly passed him by. It was difficult not to notice her; she was simply stunning: tall and slender with big blue eyes the color of a Texas sky on a summer day, and a milky white complexion with cheeks dusted the color of a pale pink rose.

She darted up the front of the church steps and interrupted one of the Sisters who was packing the decorations that had adorned the church during Advent, the Celebration of Christ's birth. "Excuse me, Sister, can you direct me to the church office?" The Sister smiled as she greeted the young woman holding the infant that was swaddled in a delicate white blanket. "It's around the corner to the left side, just down that pathway," she said.

My mother bowed her head. "Thank you, Sister, have a blessed day." She then walked down the pathway as directed and found the entrance to the church office. There was a big red door with a brown wooden crucifix on it, and a sign above the doorknob that said Church Office. She entered and, seeing no one, rang the bell on the reception desk. A few minutes later an elderly woman appeared and greeted her. "May I help you, dear?" My mother replied, "I am here to talk with Father to arrange for my daughter's baptism." Just then, I started to cry, and my mother reached into her handbag for a pacifier. She began singing to me, and I closed my eyes and fell back to sleep.

The woman smiled at my mother and handed her a clipboard with papers to complete for my baptismal certificate. "Once you have completed the forms, Father will meet with you to make the arrangements," said the volunteer. My mother placed her handbag on the counter, but there was no place to lay me down. Seeing my mother's dilemma, the volunteer offered to hold me. "What an angel," she said as she gently rocked me back and forth. "She's my Christmas angel," beamed my mother. "She was due Christmas Eve, but the doctor had family in town, so he decided to bring her in early. She was born on December 21st." My mother spent a few minutes filling out all the information needed on the forms and placed the clipboard on the reception desk. The volunteer handed me back to my mother and escorted her to Father's office.

The Father, a distinguished-looking middle-aged man wearing a neatly pressed priest's frock, greeted my mother warmly and invited her to be seated across from his desk. He offered her a cup of tea, then seated himself behind the desk and began reviewing the forms. My mother sipped the tea and gently rocked me on her lap.

After rifling through the paperwork, the priest paused, and his demeanor suddenly changed. "You were not married in the Church?" he asked.

"No, Father, my husband was divorced, and we were not permitted to be married in the Church," my mother answered with sincere honesty.

"Is he Catholic?" asked the priest.

"No, Father, he is atheist," my mother replied quietly.

Father raised his eyebrows and sat silently in contemplation for several more moments, then he shook his head. "Your child may not be baptized in the Church. She was born outside of the sacrament of marriage, and there is little hope she will be raised as a Catholic."

My mother sat across from Father's desk, stunned, with tears suddenly filling her eyes. "But, Father, she must have the sacrament, or she will not receive the Holy Spirit."

Father put his hand up to silence her and raised his voice to make the point. "Your marriage was not recognized by the Church. I cannot baptize this child; there is nothing more to discuss. You should leave."

My mother picked up her handbag, lifted me into her arms, and fled the office with tears streaming down her face as she made her way back to her car. A light rain was falling, now. She placed me in my car seat and tucked the blanket around me. She then ran to the driver's seat, pulled a handkerchief from her pocketbook, dried her tears, started the ignition, looked back at me, and swore, "I will have you baptized, my little angel. I promise."

Several weeks later, my mother walked up the steps of a beautiful little Episcopal church with my grandparents, with me sleeping peacefully in her arms. She sat in the wooden pew by the baptismal font as several other babies were baptized. Then it was time for me to be baptized. My mother handed me to the minister, and he sprinkled water on my head and said, "I baptize you, Jennifer, in the name of the Father, and of the Son, and of the Holy Ghost. Amen."

My mother cried as she told me the story of why I had not been baptized in the Catholic Church but instead in the Episcopal one. Apparently, my lack of a Catholic baptism was either unknown or had been overlooked by the priest at Saint John the Baptist Church, where I had made my First Holy Communion. My grandparents knew it, but they were determined to raise us in the Catholic Church, and they must have felt my Episcopalian baptism was good enough in the eyes of God, so they hadn't said anything.

After learning that my mother's marriage had not been blessed by the Church, I essentially felt as though I was a bastard in the Church's eyes, in that my parent's marriage had not been blessed by the Church. My mother was a good woman; she took good care of me and raised me to be a good person. My mother explained that she felt it was important to have her marriage to my stepfather receive the blessing of the Church. She told me I was old enough to make my own decision, but if I wanted to be confirmed in the Church, I would need to do as Father Tulio said, and be baptized in the Church.

I was conflicted, and the matter weighed heavily on my soul, but I eventually resolved that my birth circumstances were not my fault and that all I could do was live a good Catholic life and pray and hope that all would be well.

Father Tulio insisted that everything had to be done correctly. So my brothers and I were all baptized; we made our confessions, then received our "second" First Holy Communion; and then we received the Sacrament of Confirmation on the very same day my parents were officially married in the Church.

My stepfather shortly thereafter became an Extraordinary Minister of Holy Communion (EMHC), meaning that, as a lay person, he could assist the priest in the administration of the Holy Communion during a highly attended Mass; or when the Priest was infirm; or he could go to the home of a housebound person to bring them communion.

My grandparents occasionally joined us for Mass in our church in the mountains, and we attended Mass together with them back at Saint Matthew's in Corona on holidays. My brothers served as altar boys, and I sang in the choir. I was delighted because my entire family was finally together, happily in Church.

A year after we moved to the mountains, my stepfather had an accident and was unable to work for several months. Father Tulio offered to take up a special collection for my family. But my stepfather was a proud man and said, 'No, others need the money more than we do.' Since Dad would not accept charity, Father Tulio offered me a job cleaning the church. He offered to pay me $35 a week, quite a sum in 1977. So, at the age of 13, I started my first real job. Two days a week, I had to go to the church to dust every pew, collect and empty the trash, and vacuum the entire building. It took me nearly three hours to do my job.

Upon finishing my job, Father came by to inspect my work. He would put on a white glove and run his fingers along several pews. If he found dust on the glove, I would have to start over. I quickly learned to get good at my job. He was quite the taskmaster, but he was also a kind man, and sometimes he would give me an extra $10 and tell me it was just for me. When this happened, I had the pleasure of taking the family to dinner at Kentucky Fried Chicken. It made me happy to treat everyone, and I came to appreciate the value of hard work and diligence.

Sometimes Marguerite, my best friend from my Catechism class, would come along to work with me. I offered to split the pay with her, but she would never take a cent. She said it made her happy that she could be of help. We didn't have much in the way of material things, but it was a happy time for me. We had only one car, and because Mom worked long hours, she wasn't able to pick me up. So, after cleaning the church, I often walked home a mile and a half through the woods, on my own. I enjoyed the feeling of independence my job gave me, and I relished my time alone in the mountains to enjoy the quiet beauty of the forest and dream about my future.

Sadly, my father could no longer work at his construction job in the mountains due to his injury. So, one day, just two years after we moved to our cabin, we had another family meeting. Dad got right to the point. "I got a new job," he said. At first, I was happy. Then Mom started crying as she told us we would be moving down the mountain to a place called Redlands. I was aghast. "You mean, we are going to be flatlanders again?"

Little did I know that returning to the flatlands would be the least of the challenges my family would face. But I will be forever grateful for the blessings we received, by God's grace, to live in paradise, to have the freedom to roam the woods, explore nature, and to be part of such a wonderful parish and beautiful mountain community. The experience also taught me the value of hard work and to fully appreciate the precious opportunities we receive in life. It taught me how to weather difficult times. It taught me how families can pull together to overcome adversity. It taught me about courage. And it taught me about forgiveness, true friendship, and love. I learned that we must never take any of these things for granted. These lessons have served me well over the years.

A HARD SHAKING of the aircraft jolted everyone and made some people yell out. Jennifer awoke suddenly. The attendants asked the passengers to stow their belongings and make sure seat belts were fastened.

The turbulence lasted for several minutes, and when it was finally over, she relaxed and closed her eyes once again. More fuzzy images of the past flashed by. Perhaps the moments of air turbulence had frightened her, as her fond memories of childhood were transformed into her recurrent nightmare.

It was the day her parents had taken her to Disneyland to celebrate her excellent grades following her first year in high school. The family was having a wonderful time, but what started as one of the happiest of days turned unimaginably tragic when her stepfather had a massive heart attack in the park and was pronounced dead shortly after arriving at the hospital.

Jennifer watched in horror as her mother collapsed on the floor after learning that her husband of just four years had suddenly and unexpectedly died. He was only forty years old, and they had dreamed of growing old together. He had been in good health, so his death was totally unexpected. This tragedy shook the family to the core.

Several priests arrived at her grandparents' home that evening to console them. Father Mike, one of the young priests from her parish, stayed with Jennifer and her brothers until sunrise the next day. He held the young children as they cried in his arms, seeking to understand what had happened. He prayed with them and assured them that their father was in heaven. His kindness and reassurance comforted Jennifer on one of the most traumatic days of her life.

Jennifer awoke from her bad dream and shook off the feeling of sadness that threatened to settle in her heart. She noticed that people were once again on their computers, the turbulence having stopped. She reached down and grabbed her briefcase and took out her laptop.

Jennifer turned her laptop on, and she searched for the essay she had written for the Sisters.

Dear Sisters,

The Catholic Church gave birth to my spirituality. My spirituality has sustained me through many of life's challenges. The Church taught me about faith and the promise of eternal salvation. While I loved being Catholic, I left the Church in my twenties, when I learned the truth about my brothers having been molested by a priest. While the abuse my brothers endured was horrible, the events that followed our reporting of the abuse devastated my family and challenged everything I was taught to believe, literally destroying my faith in the Church.

I have struggled with all that has happened for decades, but I never lost my belief in God. In fact, I visited many churches and places of worship over the years. I even spent two years living part-time in an ashram, immersing myself in the study of meditation and the mind-body connection.

I believe these experiences have brought me closer to God and have helped me understand what a great gift Christ's teaching of hope, love, and forgiveness is to our world. I look at my life and all the blessings I have received, and I feel it is time for me to give back; to serve a higher purpose. I wish to bring my skills and all that I have learned to your community, to serve Christ and help people learn to forgive one another and bring God's grace into their lives, as it has been brought into mine.

I wish to continue in my work through the Church, dedicating my life to advancing the health and welfare of His people.

Jennifer wondered if the Sisters would understand and empathize with the pain she and her family had experienced from the many times they had been betrayed by the Church. The Church, with its own sins, moral absolutes, and outdated traditions, had caused her to question her faith and all that she believed. She had such mixed feelings of anger and grief, which conflicted with all the wonderful feelings she had about the Church—the community of Christ, the love and charity of her fellow parishioners, the beauty of the Mass, the sacrifice and dedication of the clergy, the service of the nuns, and the absolute faith and love her grandparents had for the Church.

She thought of the joy she felt the moment she dedicated her life completely to Christ. How could she explain to the Sisters what she didn't even understand herself? Jennifer sat calmly in her airplane seat, slowly breathing in and out, trying to understand it all. She thought about Stephen, and she felt a sense of sadness overcome her. What would she do now that their relationship had ended? Was now the time to pursue her calling? She had a lot to think about over the next several hours.

As the plane soared high above the clouds, Jennifer drifted off to sleep.

12

"Excuse me ma'am, excuse me," a voice kept repeating. Jennifer awoke feeling disoriented, then realized a stewardess was tapping her shoulder and talking to her. "I'm sorry, ma'am, but this gentleman needs a new seat. His tray broke, and we need to have him sit here." The flight attendant was talking to Jennifer as she pointed to the empty seat next to her.

Jennifer looked down the aisle and noticed there were a few other empty seats. "Oh...I see some seats farther up." There was an awkward silence as the flight attendant just stood there, waiting for Jennifer to acquiesce.

Not wanting to make the situation worse, the fellow with the attendant leaned toward Jennifer and asked, "May I sit here, please?"

Jennifer stared at the guy and the flight attendant for a moment, wishing they could hear her inner voice: *Seriously, can't you see I'm having a moment?* After realizing that neither of them seemed to recognize her discomfort, she conceded and moved her things off the seat.

The flight attendant rearranged the overhead bin as the guy returned to his former seat to retrieve his bag. He came back a minute later, placed a small suitcase in the overhead and another bag under the seat in front of him, and settled in.

The gentleman retrieved a book from his bag and, in doing so, he noticed the fatigue and stress in Jennifer's eyes and face. With intuitive concern, he looked at her and offered, "I don't wish to intrude, but you seem a bit sad. I have a big shoulder, and I'm a good listener. Let me know if you want to share whatever is bothering you."

Jennifer could not believe that this person who invaded her space seemed so forward in asking her talk when he didn't even know her. She stared at him for a moment as she thought, "Who is this guy?" But at the same time, she wondered how he could have been so perceptive as to see she was so upset.

She struggled to smile back at him. After several moments of silence, she decided to say something as simple as possible. "It's been a difficult day. I just got some bad news. I'll be okay."

The gentleman did not give up easily. "If you change your mind, I'll be here to listen. My name is Gabriel, but my friends call me Gabe," the gentleman said as he extended his hand.

She shook the young man's hand, "Hi. I'm Jennifer." Then there was an awkward silence, and she added, "I don't mean to be rude, but I'm quite tired, I think I need to close my eyes and rest a bit." She turned back to the window and pulled the blanket over her head.

"No worries, rest well," Gabe said as he opened his book and began reading. A few moments later he glanced over at the woman sleeping fitfully next to him, wondering what might have caused her such sadness.

13

As the plane continued the long flight over the US, Canada and across the vast Atlantic Ocean, the skies blackened, and faint stars began appearing. The cabin was dark, and nearly everyone was relaxing, watching movies, or sleeping. A flight attendant announced over the intercom that dinner would soon be served. The lights flickered on, waking those who would have preferred to stay asleep. Jennifer unwrapped herself from under her blanket; she stretched and pulled out her phone to check the time.

Turning to her seatmate, she felt a little guilty and offered him some small talk. "I can't believe we've been airborne for only three hours. I slept pretty hard," she remarked.

Gabe stretched and began unlocking his food tray. "Me too. But looks like it's time for dinner. I'm famished," he said, his voice sounding reassuring.

The food cart approached their row, and the flight attendant leaned in. "Would you care for chicken or steak?"

Jennifer thought for a quick second. "Chicken, please."

The flight attendant handed her a tray tightly packed with small containers of food that smelled good. "And you, sir?"

Gabe looked at her and gently said, "Actually, I reserved a vegetarian plate."

The attendant's memory was refreshed, "Ah, yes. You changed your seat. I'll ask my crewmate to bring it to you in just a moment." A minute later, Gabe's meal arrived, and he thanked her. The flight attendant departed.

Jennifer said a silent prayer and removed the plastic cover from her food tray and began to eat. Sitting next to someone while eating had the effect of opening her up a little more to talking. She took a bite of food and looked over to her seatmate. "I'm sorry about before. I didn't mean to be so...well..."

Gabe could tell that his once-sullen traveling partner seemed a bit better now that she had some sleep. "No worries," he interrupted. Gabe attempted to make small talk. "Are you going to Germany for the holiday?"

"No, I'm actually headed to Italy. I change flights in Dusseldorf. It's my brother's birthday, and I decided to treat him to a trip to the Vatican. It's sort of a combined birthday and Christmas gift."

"That's kind of you. I wish someone was paying for my trip: can I be your brother?"

Jennifer laughed, "Sure, why not? But I do have an ulterior motive.

"We're going to see the Pope!" Jennifer explained.

"The Pope? That would be remarkable," said Gabe.

"I'm sure everyone who travels to Rome wants to see him."

Jennifer laughed, "Indeed, he has become quite the celebrity."

Gabe continued, "You know, I really like this Pope. He seems like such a cool guy."

"I believe he is. Keep your fingers crossed for me," Jennifer replied.

"I will." Gabe looked at Jennifer and felt more comfortable asking her again. "I don't want to intrude, but you seemed so sad; do you want to talk about whatever is bothering you?"

"It's just been a tough day for me," Jennifer said, offering him a tad more detail. As she thought for a minute, her hesitation obvious, he interjected, "Well, I'm here if you want to share."

Jennifer took a bite of her chicken and finished chewing it. "I just needed a little space to work some things out."

He nodded his understanding. "If you need space, I could find some room in an overhead bin...or perhaps the seat pocket?" His humor was disarming. She laughed and looked at his kind face.

"Thank you. I just, well, I just broke up with my boyfriend." She grabbed the plastic cover and put it back on her unfinished meal. There was something about Gabe's kindness that encouraged her to keep talking, all the while fighting back the tears that were gathering in her eyes while she spoke. "We broke up this morning," she continued. Her voice went silent for a moment, and as she turned to Gabe, she saw he had placed his hand on his chest, as though he could feel her pain.

"I'm so sorry," he said.

Jennifer revealed her story, now grateful to have someone to share it with. As she searched for where to begin, her mind retreated to the time and place where she first met Stephen. "We met at work. He's brilliant, charming, engaging, and attractive." Just then, the flight attendants arrived to clear the plates and ask passengers if they'd like a drink.

Jennifer ordered hot chocolate. Gabe reached for his backpack and removed a small white paper deli bag and placed it on his tray. "I brought some brownies I made. Would you like one?"

"Thank you, I love chocolate," Jennifer replied as she pointed to her cup of hot chocolate. Gabe placed a brownie on a napkin and put it on her tray.

Without hesitation, she bit into the brownie and savored its rich, creamy texture. "This...is really...amazing," she managed to get out while chewing.

"I'm glad you like it," he beamed.

Gabe looked over the rims of his glasses at Jennifer. "You know, email is not a great way to communicate in a relationship. You should talk with your boyfriend when you get back to Los Angeles."

Jennifer shook her head. "I don't think it is going to work; he was very clear," she said with determination. "Besides, I think I'm meant to take another path with my life."

Gabe waited, as it seemed that Jennifer might say more. "Before I met him, I was planning to become a nun."

She searched for his reaction and was not surprised when he replied with shock.

"Really, a nun? Like convents and habits and the whole thing?" he said, his hands gesturing the shape of a habit over his head.

Jennifer laughed. "Not exactly. Most nuns don't wear habits anymore."

"So, what happened to your plan?" he asked for clarification.

"You know, it isn't as easy to become a nun as one might think." Then she added. "The first convent I applied to said I was too old. Then, I just hit one roadblock after another."

Gabe looked at Jennifer with surprise on his face. "You can't be too old to be a nun?"

"Thank you, but I'm probably old enough to be your mom. I just turned 52," she admitted.

"No way," said Gabe, a look of utter shock on his face. "You don't look that old," he added.

Jennifer laughed. Gabe looked to be in his early thirties, and she thought it funny that he commented that 52 was old. Gabe thought for a moment. "It seems strange to have an age limit to serve God," he remarked.

"I agree, a few weeks after I received my rejection letter, I talked with a priest, but he didn't give me much encouragement. I asked him if he would be my spiritual advisor, but he declined. He said that he didn't have much time due to his mission work," Jennifer recounted.

"That must have been very frustrating," said Gabe as he listened to Jennifer's story.

"It was, but I didn't give up. I reached out to the Mother Abbess of the Sisters of Mercy order that serves the Catholic Church in my hometown. I asked her if I could meet with her. But again, I was turned down. She told me she was working on closing her order in Redlands and moving all the Sisters, who were quite elderly, to a home in Ireland. She just didn't have time to add anything to her plate. She encouraged me to reach out to the Sisters of Mercy of the Americas. So, I was back to square one."

"Well, maybe God had other plans for you," Gabe said wisely.

Jennifer nodded in agreement, "I thought perhaps I had misinterpreted my calling. But then, I thought to give it one more try. A few weeks later I called the Mother Abbess again, and she gave me a phone number for one of the senior Sisters in the Sisters of Mercy convent in Northern California. I called her and set up a time to meet when she was traveling to LA, but I got ill, and we missed each other," Jennifer said with exasperation.

"I don't think I know anyone who ever contemplated becoming a nun," said Gabe.

"Well, honestly, I wasn't sure what to do next. I knew I needed to find a spiritual advisor to help me on my path. I reached out to a friend of mine, a very spiritual man, and was referred to Pastor Dan Smith, an Adventist minister."

Gabe was puzzled. "Adventist? I haven't heard of that."

"It's a Christian religion, with Protestant origins. Pastor Dan and I talked several times, and I began to study with him.

I thought seriously about becoming Adventist and asked if Pastor Dan would ordain me as a deaconess. He agreed, but during our studies together, something he said gave me second thoughts," said Jennifer.

She thought back to her time with Pastor Dan as she recounted her story, looking off into the distance. "I explained to him that I believed that, as a deaconess, I would commit to a life of celibacy; that I would remain unmarried so I'd be free to follow Christ's will. I would make a commitment to put Christ first in all aspects of my life. But then he asked me a simple question: 'What if you meet someone?' When I hesitated, he looked at me and simply said, 'Jennifer, there are many ways to serve Christ. I just want you to be sure this is what you want for your life.'"

"After our meeting, I did a lot of soul-searching. And, while I felt a strong calling to serve in a life of ministry, there was just one little problem."

Gabe smiled as he raised his eyebrows, "Let me guess: Stephen?"

Jennifer nodded and crossed her arms and put her hand on her chin as she turned to her seatmate. "Yes. I was in love with him, and I knew that I couldn't go forward with my plans to become a deaconess until I resolved my feelings for him. So, I put my religious mission on hold, and after thinking about it for several more weeks, I finally worked up the nerve to call him, and we began seeing each other. We've been together for several weeks…until this morning. And now you know the whole story."

A flight attendant pushing the beverage cart arrived at their row. They both asked for water, and the attendant poured their cups. Gabe took a sip and turned back towards Jennifer with a startlingly genuine look on his face. "I wouldn't give up if I were you. True love is a rare thing. I think you should give him another chance. You should talk with him when you get back to LA."

Jennifer smiled. "I think God has other plans for me."

"The convent?" Gabe smiled and raised his eyebrows.

"Perhaps," said Jennifer, shrugging her shoulders. "Over the past few months, I realized that I couldn't commit to becoming an Adventist. My religious beliefs as a Catholic conflicted with their teachings."

"Well, you have to follow your heart. Wherever that may lead," Gabe offered. "Perhaps you shall find a way to pursue both love and your spiritual work?"

Jennifer yawned and fluffed up her pillow. "I will give it some thought, but right now, I think I need to get some more sleep." She pulled the blanket over her shoulders and, before losing her eyes, she continued, "Thanks, Gabe, for being such a good listener. I do feel better."

Gabe took a book out of his backpack and then looked at his new friend. "My pleasure. Sleep well."

14

THE LIGHTS in the cabin came on as an announcement was made; breakfast would be served shortly. Jennifer woke up, but Gabe was still sound asleep. She nudged him. "Gabe, time for breakfast." His eyes squinted open and he stretched his arms.

"Wow, its morning already," Gabe said as he blinked several times.

"Yep, time to start a new day," Jennifer said.

"Time is going by quickly," Gabe commented. The flight attendants passed by with their carts and served Jennifer and Gabe their breakfast. They opened their food containers, and Jennifer closed her eyes and said a prayer and began to eat.

Gabe looked at Jennifer intently. "Have you always been so religious?"

"That's a long story," Jennifer said, rolling her eyes.

"Well, we still have at least a couple of hours and I've finished with my book, so do tell."

Jennifer took a deep breath and shrugged her shoulders, not sure what to say.

"Come on, we've come this far. Don't hold out on me, I'm really curious," said Gabe.

"Okay, if you insist." Jennifer took a few bites of her breakfast. "I grew up in a devoutly Catholic family. But I left the Church in my 20s and began to explore other faiths."

"I can relate to that," Gabe said, nodding his head and adding, "A lot of people reject stuff they grew up with when they get to their early 20s. I was raised in a traditional Jewish family, but I've read a lot about Buddhism and it seems to make a lot of sense to me."

"I studied Buddhism and Hinduism," Jennifer said, then added: "I even lived part-time in an ashram in Oregon."

"That must have been really interesting. What was it like?" Gabe asked.

"It was a blast, and I learned a great deal about myself. I enjoyed the routine and shared responsibility of communal living. I think the experience played a role in my desire to join a convent," Jennifer said, as she reflected on her time at the ashram. She sat quietly for a few moments, picking at her breakfast. "But as much as I enjoyed my time with them, it never quite felt like my spiritual home. I didn't realize it at the time, but my Catholic roots were very deep."

"Is that when you decided to rejoin the Catholic Church?" asked Gabe.

"That happened a few years later, actually, when I was going through a difficult personal experience. I realized I had to confront that problem for myself, but this event helped me confront the original trauma that had separated me from the Church."

Gabe's eyes grew large, and he looked at Jennifer curiously. "Trauma? What do you mean?"

Jennifer took a deep breath, then answered, aware that she was about to release her secrets to a stranger. "I learned in my mid-twenties that both of my brothers had been molested by our parish priest when they were young boys."

Gabe put his hand over his mouth. "That must have been awful!"

"It was. The priest was a close friend of our family; someone we completely trusted. But the worst part was how the Church sought to cover up the incident, and then turn the tables on my family. They actually tried to blame my mother."

Gabe gasped, "That must have been very painful for her!"

"It was, and she felt terrible. But it wasn't her fault; she had no idea what had happened. We didn't learn of their abuse until they were older, when my brother Patrick ran into trouble and got arrested. My mother was ashamed and refused to visit or even write to him. My brother Michael knew Patrick was distraught and that he needed support. He asked me if I would help change my mother's mind. He arranged for the three of us to have lunch together to ask her to reconsider," Jennifer said, as she thought back on the day that so changed her life.

"We met for lunch at the Sizzler, in Redlands. I remember it like it was yesterday. Michael told us that Patrick was suicidal, and he pleaded with her: 'Please, Mom, he is really scared, and he needs his family.'

"But my mother shook her head. 'Sorry, Michael, I won't go to that place. I can't accept his poor choices.' Then Michael yelled at her: 'It's not his fault, you don't know what happened to Patrick.' She looked up at Michael with anger in her eyes. 'There's no excuse for what he did.'

Michael got quiet, then said, 'Yes, there is. Patrick—actually, we—were both abused by Father Howard when we were little.' My mother sat up in her chair with a look of disbelief. She couldn't speak. I was aghast and asked my brother, 'What do you mean, you were abused by Father Howard?'"

Jennifer sat quietly for a few minutes, composing herself as she felt tears welling in her eyes as she recalled the story.

Gabe handed Jennifer some Kleenex. "Are you okay?"

Jennifer nodded and continued, "Michael sat with a stony look on his face, then he told us the story. 'He molested us for years. Every time we went on fishing trips with him, and even the times when we all traveled to Las Vegas with Grandma and Grandpa. Remember, we stayed in his room. He would send one of us to the pool, while he... And it happened again when Patrick was sent to Texas, to stay with Father at the Rectory.' Michael, got emotional and couldn't continue. My mother turned white as a ghost. I couldn't believe what he was saying, yet I knew it had to be true. It explained so much." As Jennifer spoke, she had a haunted look on her face as she recalled the events of that day.

Gabe looked at Jennifer in stunned silence. "That must have been horrible for you and your mother, what did you do?"

Jennifer continued, "My mother could barely move, so I drove her home. Then I went home and called the Diocese and asked for Father Mike's number."

Gabe asked, "Who is Father Mike?"

"He was a young priest at the church where we grew up. He had been very kind to our family. I called him because I knew he was working in prison ministry. I told him what we had learned, and that Patrick was in jail. I asked him if he would go see Patrick and talk to him. I thought he might be able to help him in some way," Jennifer said, expressing her hope.

"Did he help?" Gabe asked with serious intent.

She continued, "He informed me that he had to report the abuse to the Church officials and he said he would do whatever he could to help us. He did visit Patrick, and then a few days later we had a visit from two priests from the Diocese. They called me to schedule a time to meet with our family. We agreed to meet with them and they came to my home. At first, they seemed very concerned as we shared our story. Then, they asked to speak alone with Michael.

"Before they left, they gave me their cards and told me that if we had any questions, we should feel free to call them. They said they would be investigating the matter, and that they would be in touch with us in a few weeks. They also asked us to provide my grandparents' contact information. I told them we didn't want my grandparents involved. They had both been very close to Father Howard, and I knew that this revelation would destroy them. I shared that my grandparents were quite elderly, and that my grandmother had heart problems. I told the priests that we would be happy to help with the investigation, but to please leave our grandparents alone. They agreed to honor our wishes."

Gabe spoke up. "That's totally understandable; that kind of news would be devastating for my grandparents—for anyone's family, for that matter."

Jennifer continued on with her story. "Well, several days later, I received a call from my grandfather. The two priests who had visited with us flew to Florida and met with my grandparents at their home. They had no idea what the meeting was about. When the priests arrived, they informed them that they were lawyers investigating allegations my brothers had made against Father Howard."

Gabe interjected. "They were lawyers? I thought you said they were priests!"

"That's what I thought, but my grandfather told me that the two priests were actually lawyers for the Church. I remember my grandfather was so angry with me. 'What's this all about Jennifer?' he asked me in an accusatory tone.

"I told my grandfather what had happened: that I had called Father Mike for help, and that the two priests had come to visit us and said they would help, but I didn't know they were lawyers. My grandfather was very worried about my grandmother. She was having heart problems, and their visit was very distressing to her.

"I told my grandfather how sorry I was, and how all I wanted to do was spare them pain. But he replied to me, 'You should have called me so we could be better prepared to deal with this.'

"'Yes, Grandpa. I'm so sorry,' I said.

'Well, we answered their questions. They asked us if the boys had ever been sent alone to the rectory. We told them the truth: that yes, they had each stayed with Father Howard at the rectory several times to go on fishing trips. Is that when this happened?'

'Yes, Grandpa.'

'When did you learn about this?' he asked me.

"I told him that Michael had just told us and that we didn't want to upset them, so we asked the priests—uh, the lawyers—not to contact them. To tell you the truth, Gabe, I was shocked that they didn't honor our request."

"It must have been very difficult for your grandparents," said Gabe.

"It was, but it got worse; much worse. The two priests visited Patrick in jail. They accused him of lying. They told him they believed he was making up the story to get out of trouble, and that he should be a real man and accept responsibility for his actions. They said, 'It's no wonder you are so depressed; Father Howard is a good priest, and you are ruining his life with your accusations. They told him, 'You should repent and pray that God forgives you of your sins for shifting the blame for your actions onto such a good man of the Church.'

"Patrick was distraught. He explained that he wasn't the one who had reported the abuse, and he didn't want to cause any trouble. They prayed with him and asked God to have mercy on him and help him accept accountability for his actions. Their visit left him feeling even more ashamed. When I found out what they had done, I got very angry. I wanted to protect my family. And once I knew that they had lawyers involved, I decided to consult an attorney, who referred us to another law firm that handled these types of cases. We met with them, and they decided to take my brothers' case."

"It's good that you got some help. I'm sure it was all very overwhelming," said Gabe.

"It was actually a horrible experience. We had to go through a lot of legal depositions, where they asked my brothers intimate details about every aspect of their sexual history. They asked if my brothers were gay; they accused them of conspiring to blackmail Father Howard. It went on and on. It was as though they were trying to shame them into silence. During my mother's deposition, they made her feel like it was all her fault. She was sick for months afterward. And, what's worse is that she actually started to believe it was her fault; that she should have known. The attorney we were working with seemed like he was just out to make a name for himself. He didn't seem to really care about my brothers..."

Gabe interjected: "I can't believe they were so callous and that they actually tried to blame your mother for what happened."

Jennifer looked away and said, "I wish I had never made that phone call asking for help. I later learned that it was common practice for how some of the leadership in the Church handled abuse allegations in those days. They used all kinds of intimidation tactics to get people to back down and even recant. And it worked on us. When they were getting ready to do depositions with my grandparents, my brothers didn't want to put them through such a painful experience. So they decided to settle rather than drag out the process."

Gabe looked at Jennifer and said, "I hope they got a good settlement."

"Nope, they each ended up with just a few thousand dollars for some counseling. But it was never about money. We just wanted enough to get help for my brothers," Jennifer said as she looked out the window and dabbed her eyes with her napkin.

Gabe became concerned and he asked, "Are you okay?"

Jennifer composed herself. "It tore me up to see my brothers in such pain, and there was nothing I could do. And, in all honesty, it affected me, too. I remember sometimes, when Father Howard gave me communion, his fingers would touch my lips as he placed the wafer on my tongue—those same fingers he used to molest my little brothers. It just made me sick inside. I stopped going to church. It was like a light in my soul had been extinguished."

"I'm so sorry to hear. Are your brothers okay, now?" Gabe asked with a look of genuine pity on his face.

"No, they're not. They were deeply damaged. Patrick has PTSD, and he has a difficult time trusting people; his second marriage is falling apart. On top of the emotional trauma, two years after the matter was settled, Michael got cancer, and he is disabled from the effects of his cancer treatment. He has a lot of pain, both physical and emotional. He once told me he believed God had abandoned him."

Gabe looked as though he was going to cry. "That's very sad."

Jennifer took a moment to reflect, then continued: "They were such bright children; so full of life and potential. Neither of them ever had a chance," Jennifer said almost to herself as she looked out the window. She felt deep sorrow for what happened to her brothers.

"After all that happened to your family, why did you go back to the Catholic Church?" asked Gabe.

"I believe it was a combination of things. I saw a program on Pope Francis. He decreed an extraordinary Jubilee, called the Year of Mercy that began in November, 2015. He spoke about forgiveness, and made several public apologies for the past sins of the Church. He said he would be forming a special commission to help victims, and he would be enforcing a zero-tolerance policy on clergy sexual abuse. I was intrigued, and I began to think about going to back to Church again."

"Yes, I remember when the Pope apologized for the clergy sexual abuse problem. It made international headlines. So, that's what brought you back to church?" Gabe asked.

"My grandmother was also my Godmother, and she

would often pray to the Blessed Virgin to watch over me. She told me that when I was troubled, I should pray to the Blessed Virgin for her intervention. Last year I was struggling with a challenge at work, and I didn't know what to do. So, I borrowed my grandmother's rosary from my mother, and I went to Church. I was immediately drawn to the statue of Mary. I said the rosary and I prayed for clarity on the matter."

Gabe looked at Jennifer curiously. "In the Jewish faith, one's parents are responsible for their children's spiritual development. My mother took her role as our spiritual advisor pretty seriously, too. So did you get the answer you expected?" asked Gabe.

"To be honest, I wasn't sure what to expect," Jennifer replied. "But after praying to the Blessed Virgin, I did resolve my issue, and I came to a place of peace with the situation. Then while I was in the church, memories of all the masses I had attended came flooding back to me. It was like a waterfall. I realized how much I missed being Catholic. I came to realize that what had happened to my family was an act of sin on behalf of just one man who was a priest. It was a grievous sin. However, priests are just as vulnerable to evil and sin as the rest of us."

"That's true, we're all human," said Gabe matter-of-factly.

"I realized I had allowed a man who sinned and my anger at the way we were treated to come between me and my faith, and that was wrong. Deep inside, I knew that the priests who defended Father Howard were trying to preserve the reputation of the Church. I believe they thought they were doing the right thing at the time. Once I understood this, the only thing I could do was to forgive them. When I let go of the anger and shame, it was as though a huge burden had been lifted off my shoulders. The pain just melted away and I felt such peace. It was like being reborn, in a way. I felt I had discovered the Church and the real meaning of my faith for the first time."

Gabe was speechless. He truly didn't know what to say, so he remained quiet.

"That's when I had the calling to become nun. I wanted to help others reconcile to their faith. I wanted to help save souls."

Gabe looked at Jennifer with compassion. "That's an incredible story," he said.

"It gets better. I faxed Pope Francis a letter last week, explaining all that had transpired, and asked if he would meet with me. And a few days later, I received the invitation from his office to come to the General Audience. It said there may be a brief encounter with him following the service. I don't know if we'll actually get to meet him, but I'm hopeful." Jennifer returned to her tray of food and nibbled a bit of the cold omelet.

"Wow, he actually responded. That must have been some letter you wrote!" exclaimed Gabe.

Jennifer nodded. "It was six pages. The words just poured out of me. It was as though God was writing to the Pope through me. I never experienced anything like it."

Gabe looked at Jennifer with hope. "If you get to see him, what are you expecting?"

"I have a gift for him," Jennifer smiled as she thought of the gift nestled in the box in her backpack. She added, "And, I'm hoping it will help my brother see that the Pope is sincere in his efforts to fix the Church."

"Well, I hope you do get to see him, though I don't know if I could be so forgiving. I'm impressed by what you are doing."

Jennifer looked back at Gabe shyly. "Thanks, you've been a great seatmate." She felt a bit embarrassed, and decided to change the subject. "I feel I've been a bit selfish; I really haven't learned anything at all about you, Gabe. Now it's your turn. What brings you on this trip?" Jennifer asked.

Gabe spread butter and jam on his bread. "I'm headed to Berlin, where I'm visiting friends for the holidays."

Jennifer was genuinely delighted for him. "That sounds wonderful. I've never been to Berlin."

Gabe was finishing up his breakfast. "It's beautiful this time of year. I love Europe. I'm working on getting a job in Switzerland, so I can be closer to my friends and family. But it has been very difficult."

"That sounds exciting. What's keeping you back?"

"I need to get a permit to work in the EU," Gabe said.

"What kind of work do you do?"

Gabe swallowed, then he said, "I work as the pastry chef at The Grille, in Westwood."

Jennifer stopped chewing. She looked shocked as she turned to Gabe and stared at him with intensity. Gabe was curious and taken aback by her reaction.

"Do you know of it?" He looked at her with a questioning gaze.

Jennifer looked dumbfounded as she said, with awe in her voice, "It's a wonderful place. It's the very restaurant where I fell in love with Stephen at a business dinner we were both attending!"

"Wow, that's a coincidence!" Gabe exclaimed.

"It was last April 8th. I remember the date because it was my brother's birthday."

"Well, I just started working there a few months ago. Perhaps when you get back to LA, you can come in and I'll make you a special desert," said Gabe.

"That would be nice," Jennifer said. Then she sat, speechless. She was stunned by the statistical probability of meeting someone on this plane who had been accidentally reseated next to her, who then turned out to work at the very same place where she had fallen in love for the first time in eight years. And she had just spent hours talking with him about the deepest secrets of her life and family. It felt like an astonishing connection. What did it mean?

The attendant who had reseated Gabe arrived at Jennifer's row to gather their food trays. Seeing Jennifer now smiling, she leaned in to them. "I'm so happy to see the seating arrangements worked out."

Jennifer nodded and smiled, saying, "Yes, it's been unexpectedly wonderful." The attendant retrieved their food trays and moved to the next row.

Jennifer immediately put her tray table back up in its stowed position and reached for her briefcase under the seat in front of her. She removed her laptop from the bag.

Gabe took notice, so Jennifer quickly said, "Thanks for listening to me for so long. I have some work to do before we land. Ok?"

Gabe understood and reached into his backpack and took out his earphones. "No worries. I'll catch a movie before landing. Let's see what the options are. *Jaws* or *Risky Business*? Hmm, *Jaws* ought to keep me awake."

15

GABE PLUGGED IN his earphones and launched the movie. Jennifer stared at her computer screen, deep in thought, her fingers ready to type out an email, though she was not sure what to say.

When she received Stephen's email that he didn't want to pursue a serious relationship, Jennifer thought that if she was to meet the Pope, she might ask him to allow her to start her own order, after all. She now believed that perhaps this was God's way of telling her she should give the relationship more time.

She began to write "Dear Stephen," and then she stopped. What to write from there was unclear. She typed a phrase, erased it, typed another, and erased that. Her inner voice was talking a mile a minute, yet she could not decipher the words. She had so many feelings that she needed to process.

She decided that she needed to think more clearly about what to write, this time. She closed her laptop and put it away, and with a long yawn, curled up and fell back to sleep, leaving Gabe to his movie.

In its last hour of flight, the plane flew south across the vast European continent. Sunlight began infiltrating the cabin, and passengers opened their window shades, awestruck by the beautiful dawn sunlight on Christmas Day. It was early morning in Germany, where Jennifer would need to change planes for Italy after a short layover. The pilot spoke calmly over the intercom in a pleasant German accent. "Good morning, ladies and gentlemen. We are preparing for our descent into Dusseldorf. We should be touching down in about thirty minutes. Thank you for choosing Air Berlin for your travel, it's been a pleasure serving you. We wish you a pleasant holiday wherever your travels may take you."

The plane descended through thin clouds. Jennifer stared out the window, reflecting on her encounter with Gabe. She knew that meeting him may have appeared to be just an accidental encounter, but the synchronicity of his working at the place where she had fallen in love was too intriguing to believe it was a simple accident. It truly felt like a message from God. We make of such coincidences whatever we may wish to make of them, but to her, Gabe had offered a new perspective: that she could both have her relationship and pursue her missionary work.

The historic city of Dusseldorf came into view as the plane glided earthwards and landed smoothly. Once at the gate, Jennifer and Gabe gathered their things and stood up to wait for passengers ahead of them to disembark. Gabe looked at his watch and felt it was a good time to say his farewells.

"Well, looks like we arrived on time. It was great getting to know you, Jennifer. I hope you find the right path that makes you happy and that everything turns out well for your brothers."

Jennifer appreciated his sincere expression of goodwill. "Thank you, Gabe, for everything—for listening, for being there, and for making such great brownies." They laughed together just as it was their turn to exit the cabin.

Inside the terminal, Gabe gave Jennifer a hug. "I'll pray for you," he said.

"Thanks; and Gabe, you do have great shoulders," Jennifer replied in a teasing tone as she squeezed his shoulders. Gabe laughed as he understood her meaning. Then they looked at each other a last moment, a deep connection having formed between them when just ten hours ago they were complete strangers.

"Whatever you do, follow your heart," he said.

"I will. I promise. I hope you have a wonderful time with your friends."

They both walked separately down the long corridor to the central terminal and headed in opposite directions, waving goodbye. Now on her own, Jennifer checked the monitor for her departing flight to Milan and saw she had only a small amount of time; not enough to write the email she was eager to produce. Los Angeles was nine hours behind her, so he was probably asleep, anyway, but she vowed to write it on the next plane and send it from Milan.

16

IMMEDIATELY AFTER BOARDING her next flight to Milan, Jennifer reached for her laptop, opened it, and began to write the email she wanted to send. She kept it a simple, straight-from-the-heart message, asking Stephen to give their relationship another chance.

With no internet on the plane and her battery light flashing "low power," she closed her computer and stowed it in her bag. Deep in thought, she stared out the window. Europe just had a very different feeling than the US. Before she knew it, the plane descended into Milan and she disembarked, where she was directed to customs. She moved through the line on automatic pilot, deep in thought, hardly noticing her passport being stamped for entry. Once she was cleared, she made her way to the baggage claim to retrieve her luggage.

Mike would be waiting for her in Milan, having already been traveling in Europe for a week on his own. It was now Christmas Day, and their plan was to immediately take a train to Venice to spend a day there and then go to Rome the next day. She texted Mike "Where are you?" and a few seconds later, he replied, "about 30 minutes outside the airport."

"Okay. I'm going to see if I can rustle up some chow. I'm famished."

Jennifer spotted a small food court where she ordered a slice of real Italian pizza and a soft drink. She realized that she had time enough to send her email. She turned her attention back to her computer screen, found her email, and pressed the 'Send' button. The message was sent just in time, as her phone rang: the awaited call from Michael. They fixed a meeting place outside the terminal.

The chilled air outdoors hit Jennifer's face with a zing as she exited the terminal and looked for her brother. As soon as they spotted each other, their close emotional bond connected like electricity, and they hugged tightly. She needed to feel that family connection, after what she had been through. They made their way to the taxi stand and got into a waiting cab. "Benvenuto signore, signora," the driver said.

Jennifer looked at Michael. He had studied the language in preparation for the trip, and he said, "Ciao signore, stazione ferrovia, per favore." The Italian taxi driver nodded, confirming Michael's request: "Si signore, stazione ferroviaria."

As they rode in silence, Michael sensed that something was wrong with his sister. He glanced over at her. "Are you okay?"

Jennifer took a deep breath. She looked out the window of the taxi, admiring the rich culture around her. Finally, she answered, "I broke up with Stephen." Michael did not hesitate in his empathy for her.

"That sucks. What happened?" He took his sister in his arms and hugged her.

Feeling comforted already, she said, "I'll fill you in on the train.

"We better get our tickets; the next train leaves in fifteen minutes," Jennifer said as she looked at her watch.

Michael nodded, and the two siblings exited the taxi and headed into the train station.

17

JENNIFER AND MICHAEL admired the beauty and quaintness of the villages and the countryside as their train traveled east through Italy to Venice. Michael had taken up photography; he especially loved taking photos of the ancient buildings, churches, and temples in Rome. He spent an hour sharing all the photos he had taken, and they laughed as he told Jennifer of the run-in he'd had with a young boy who had tried to pick his pocket on the train.

"I had learned my lesson the last time I was here. When I got bumped by the small boy, I knew he would reach into my pocket. So, I grabbed his hand and said, 'Boo. Caught you.' The boy looked shocked, then smiled and turned on his charm. Can you believe, he actually had the gumption to ask me for some money for food."

"Really? What did you do next?" Jennifer said, laughing at the audacity of the boy.

"I caved. His sly smile won me over. That, and the fact that he was barefoot. I felt sorry for the little guy."

Jennifer smiled. Although he'd had a tough life, Michael had a kind heart. And, she was happy to see him smiling. It wasn't often that he let his guard down.

The train porter made an announcement, "Prossima fermata, Venezia," as he passed by Michael, who nodded a thank you. Michael hugged his sister and told her to start getting ready to exit the train.

At the station, the two descended onto a crowded platform, filled with tourists and locals going about their business.

The two siblings immediately looked for the sign to the ferry and scampered through the crowd to its mooring. They stepped onto the vaporetto with their luggage amidst a sea of global visitors speaking dozens of languages.

The spirit of Christmas descended upon them as they glided through the Venetian waterways, which were lit up in hues of green, red, and white. Jennifer turned to her brother and wrapped her arms around his shoulders as he leaned on the worn, weathered sideboards of the vaporetto. The boat made its way through the canals, swishing the water aside in small waves. Nearly every home along the canal was decorated in Christmas lights, and many had beautifully decorated Christmas trees prominently displayed in their windows. They admired the architecture, the maze of canals, and the sense of stepping into a thousand years of Western cultural history.

Jennifer's mood seemed to lighten as they traveled down the great canal. She pointed to different sites along the way, trying to remember their names from a prior trip she and her brother had taken when he had recovered from his bone marrow transplant years before.

The vaporetto slowed as it approached the dock, where men steadied the boat so passengers could safely disembark. Jennifer and her brother grabbed their luggage, and as they moved along with the other passengers, she made eye contact with the vaporetto operator and handed him some Euro, saying "Grazie." He appeared delighted, tipped his cap, and with a flirtatious smile, he said, "Una bella città per una bella signora!" (A beautiful city for a beautiful woman!). Italian men never pass up a chance, she thought.

Michael was happy to see his sister a bit more at peace. He could see at the airport that she felt terribly wounded, and he could empathize with her hurt. Jennifer had been his rock when he had cancer, and now this entire trip, planned as a vacation for the two of them, had taken on a new twist with the Pope's invitation. He knew she had done it for him.

They made their way down the dock as Michael pulled out a map and searched for their hotel. Meanwhile, Jennifer felt she was being pulled in by an invisible cultural force emanating from this astonishingly gorgeous city. She stepped away from her brother when she spotted the historic Basilica di Santa Maria della Salute, whose design and dome are among the masterpieces of 17th-century architecture. Completely bathed in Christmas lighting, it was breathtaking beyond imagination.

She stood still, in awe of the beauty and the spiritual energy she felt. She reached for her phone and began snapping photos of the Basilica. She closed her eyes, took a deep breath, and exhaled to relieve her anxieties. Her entire body felt a sense of peace.

Just as she was opening her eyes, her phone rang, and she looked to see who it was. She gasped, recognizing the number from which the call came, and she felt a sudden surge of excitement. It was Stephen. She looked over in the direction of her brother and motioned for him to wait. Walking along the dock railing, she gazed at the changing reflections of light on the waters and pressed the 'Accept Call' button.

"Hi, Doctor. How are you?" Stephen asked.

"I'm ok," she replied nervously. Her voice cracked a little as she spoke.

"Really?" the voice on the other side asked.

She took a breath and thought for a second. Gabe's words flashed through her mind, and she realized she wanted to answer him with her genuine feelings. "It was a rough trip." She knew he would get what she meant, but she added, "But today, well, it's a new day. We just arrived in Venice." Jennifer wiped a tear from her cheek as her brother looked in her direction, concern on his face. "And you?" she inquired.

Stephen's voice was upbeat. "I'm good. It's Christmas morning here; the house is bustling, the grandkids just opened their presents, and we just got back from a walk on the beach."

Jennifer could hear children in the background, and it made her smile. She closed her eyes as the ocean breeze blew in her face. With a sense of peace, she said, "I'm sorry I sent you that email."

He responded immediately. "Don't worry about that right now. We'll get together when you get back in town, and we'll talk. I want you to enjoy your time in Italy," he assured her.

She could hear he was being sincere. She felt relieved with the tone of their conversation so far. "Okay," she replied. "It's beautiful here. I'll send you pictures," Jennifer playfully added.

"Okay, you send me pictures and I'll call you in a few days. I admit, I'm a bit envious," he said, clearly smiling in his response.

"Thank you for calling. Merry Christmas," Jennifer said with a smile.

"Goodbye, Jennifer. We'll talk soon," he replied.

Jennifer didn't know what might happen. All she could do now was to put the relationship in God's hands. She put her phone back in her purse and returned to join Michael, who was still peering at the map. "I found the hotel, and we can walk from here. Then, hopefully, we can find a nice restaurant to have a real Christmas dinner," he said. Michael called one of the bag carriers to help with their larger suitcases.

"You lead the way," she said as Michael placed his arm around his sister's shoulders. The two siblings made their way down the narrow streets and walkways of Venice until they found a charming classic Venetian hotel. A young clerk welcomed them inside with "Benvenuto, signore, signora!" and Jennifer smiled gleefully, feeling she was stepping into an entirely new world.

Michael's Italian was not strong enough to conduct the check-in, so Jennifer simply spoke in English. "We have a reservation. Wortham." The clerk understood and searched the computer for their reservation. "Si, si, l'ho trovato," he said to himself, then repeated in English: "I have found your rooms.

"You have complimentary breakfast that will be served from 6:30 am to 9:30 am. Do you need a bellman for the bags?' he asked.

"Yes, thank you," said Jennifer.

Then he handed them a pen and registration slip and asked for their passports. Gesturing upstairs and using his fingers to show the number 2, he said, "La tua stanza è al secondo nivello," as he pointed to the narrow stairway and gave them the keys. Then he said, "The bellman will arrive shortly with your bags."

After freshening up, the siblings headed out with excitement to discover whatever Venice would bring them. They walked and stopped several times, simply looking in all directions and soaking in the cool evening air. "Let's take a chance and go this way," Jennifer suggested.

Michael shrugged his shoulders. "Why not?"

They made their way along the crowded sidewalks as the Christmas decorations brought everyone out into the night in Venice. Within blocks, Michael spotted a restaurant that looked open. The aroma from inside wafted out and made their stomachs growl. "If it tastes as good as it smells, I think we're in for a treat," Jennifer commented.

Inside, they were greeted by a distinguished host who bowed slightly and welcomed them in the customary Italian manner. "Benvenuto. Benvenuto, per due?" Jennifer nodded yes. "Seguimi," he said politely, leading the way to a table next to a window.

They ordered their meals, fresh handmade pasta dishes, and as they ate, Michael made small talk. Then he worked up the nerve to ask, "So, you and Stephen, are you okay?

Jennifer shrugged her shoulders. But she had a glint of hope in her eyes. "I don't know where things will wind up, but I'm glad he called."

Michael smiled, happy for his sister. "I'm sure he cares for you." Jennifer's eyes showed how grateful she was for her brother's support. After dinner, they ordered espressos and sipped them slowly, enjoying the ambiance of the charming Italian restaurant.

Michael decided that it was the right moment to ask her the question he had been mulling over for weeks. "Jennifer, I want you to know that I'm am happy that we might get to meet the Pope. But, I'm really wondering how can you forgive the Church after everything that happened?"

Jennifer sat quietly for a few moments, thinking how she would answer her brother's important question with sensitivity to his feelings. "You know, Michael, it was difficult, I prayed about it and I forgave the Church because I needed to let go of the anger and resentment I was feeling so I could be free to move on with my life."

Michael frowned, and Jennifer could sense her brother's contempt. She could not blame him. But she wanted to offer him an explanation from her heart. "Something about Pope Francis gives me great hope, Michael," she declared. "He seems to be truly sorry for everything that happened in the Church. His humbleness and commitment to service have really touched my soul. He is so different from any other Pope I have seen in my lifetime. I truly believe he will get things fixed in the Church. And, I believe the Church is headed on a new path."

Michael listened intently, absorbing her comments, but his own pain was resurfacing, as it had many times in his life. "I just don't think I will ever be able to forget what happened to me."

Jennifer let Michael's anger have its moment. Reaching out to touch his arm, she offered, "It's important to remember that forgiveness is different from condoning or forgetting what happened."

"What do you mean?" asked Michael.

"The Greek word for 'forgiveness' literally means 'to let go.' I will never excuse or forget what happened to you and Patrick and our family. Any priest who commits a crime is subject to the law of the land, and the Church should take responsibility and do whatever they can to make things right."

"What if they don't take responsibility, and the priests just go on doing what they are doing?" Michael asked.

Jennifer looked deeply into Michael's eyes and said, "Sometimes, life is not fair, and when we don't receive justice from the law, the only option is to let our anger go and leave justice to God. Anyway, I planned this trip to meet Pope Francis and give him a gift, and I'll encourage him to continue to work on this issue."

Michael was quiet as he contemplated what his sister was saying to him.

Jennifer continued, "I do understand your pain, and you have a right to be angry about what happened to you. But anger can be a poison that eats at one's soul. By holding onto your anger, you are allowing Father Howard to continue to impact your life. If you don't find a way to let go of all that rage inside of you, you will never find peace."

Michael sat looking at Jennifer in silence, not knowing what to say.

Jennifer added, "You don't have to let what happened to you control your life and rob you of your chance to be happy."

Michael sighed and downed the remainder of his cold espresso. He was clearly upset, but Jennifer hoped he might understand one more thing. "Without forgiveness, the world would be a merciless place, full of hatred and bitterness, and we would destroy one another."

Michael seemed to soften, and he listened closely to what his sister was saying. They had a deep bond, and he knew she would always look out for him.

Jennifer continued. "Who wants to live in a world with no hope? When I saw Pope Francis speak about the "sins" of the Church, I saw how sincere he was about righting the wrongs of the past. I returned to the Church because I felt there was finally a leader I could follow."

"I hope you are right, that the Pope can fix the Church." Michael looked up at Jennifer, and she saw a shadow of pain cross his eyes.

Seeing Michael's pain saddened her, and she resolved to find a way to help him, so that he too might one day find peace. He had struggled all his life with depression and anxiety, and his cancer treatment had left him in constant pain. Jennifer whispered, "Are you ok?" as she reached her hands out across the table.

After a moment, Michael reached back and clasped her hands in his. Then he smiled. "I'm okay, but I'll be even better after we find some gelato."

Jennifer smiled. "Pistachio gelato it is." Michael had developed quite a fondness for Pistachio gelato since they had made their first journey to Italy, several years ago.

Michael asked for the check, and as they waited, Jennifer decided to share another secret with Michael. "I've been working on a book about what happened to our family, and my journey over the past year."

"I can't wait to read your book," Michael said; then he winked at his sister. "I'm glad you decided to give up the idea of becoming a nun. I'm sure Stephen is glad, as well."

Jennifer rebuked her brother with mock indignation for his salacious reference: "What kind of girl do you think I am?"

Michael laughed at the look on his sister's face.

"The good kind. I'm just teasing you, Sis. Now, let's go get some gelato." His sense of humor returning made Jennifer laugh and cry at the same time.

The next morning, as they exited the hotel, the spirit of Christmas infused their souls. They marveled at the architectural wonders of the magical city on the water. Nearly every shop, house, and piazza was decorated in Christmas ornaments and colorful lights. The holiday cheer was infectious as the throngs of visitors from around the world stared in wonder at the magical city.

Jennifer and her brother found a quaint café and had some lunch, then headed off to shop. They bought holiday cards and souvenirs, took pictures, and soaked up the beautiful sights and wonderful smells that were unique to Venice. It was a special time for the two of them; a time to reconnect and play as they did when they were children"

18

THE NEXT MORNING, December 27, Jennifer and Michael waited on the Venezia Santa Lucia train station platform, preparing for the final leg of their trip to Rome and the Vatican. Jennifer turned and took one last look at Venice, then embraced her brother. "I really needed this."

Michael replied, "Me too. It's been the best birthday and Christmas ever!" The two siblings stepped quickly into the train car as the doors opened. Shortly, the bullet train accelerated smoothly, hardly making a sound. Within a minute, it felt like they were doing 150 mph on the high-speed line—and they were. Passengers shuffled calmly through the aisle, heading to the café car for coffee. Both Jennifer and Michael stared out the large window, eyeing the scenic Italian countryside and quaint villages.

Now and again, they turned to each other and exchanged a comment or an "ooh" and an "ah" as the train entered and exited various tunnels along the way, the swish of increased air pressure deafening them momentarily. Soon, a sign reading ROME informed them that the ride was nearly over.

They made eye contact, their excitement was hardly containable. An announcement confirmed their proximity: "Il treno arriverà in Roma in venti minuti. Si prega di preparare per la partenza." (The train will arrive in Rome in 20 minutes. Please prepare for arrival.)

Jennifer's eyes opened wide as she looked over to her brother. "It's been a long journey, and now I can't believe I'm actually here." She knew her time in Rome would be special, a once-in-a-lifetime event, and she felt overcome with excitement.

Once they got situated in their hotel, they decided they should visit as many sites in Rome as possible, given that they only had a few days there and so much to see. They also had to go to the Vatican to pick up their tickets, as it was not something that could be done online. They visited the Coliseum, Aventine Hill, and the Piazza Novana. The last place they managed to get in that afternoon was the Trevi Fountain, and as any visitor there knows, you are obliged to toss a coin in and wish for something. Jennifer tossed in a 2-Euro coin while most people threw in just 10, 20, or 50 centimes (cents). "My wish is expensive." Michael laughed at his sister as she watched the coin settle on the bottom of the fountain.

"Come on, sister, it's getting late," Michael said. He flagged a taxi for them, and fortunately the driver spoke some English. "Destination?" he asked Michael, looking at him from his rearview mirror.

"The Vatican, Si Prega," said Michael.

The driver nodded, "Si, Signore," and took off like the proverbial Italian race car driver. The siblings laughed as they held on tight to the door handles, bumping into one another as the cab driver zigzagged around cars, breaking hard, then accelerating at heart-stopping rates.

As the Vatican finally came into view, Jennifer scooched forward to get a good view. Their driver slowed to a stop, and said proudly, "Here is the Vatican."

Once they were in the plaza, Jennifer searched in her purse and found the paper she needed. They approached two guards smoking cigarettes in the middle of the plaza, showing it to them. One guard pointed to the bronze doors. They made their way across the great square, to their destination. There was an impressive set of ancient bronze doors that appeared to be large enough for an army to walk through.

One of the doors was open and was manned by a Vatican guard. When they approached the guard asked politely, "How may I assist you?"

"We are here to pick up the pass for the audience," Jennifer said as she handed the guard the paper from the Prefecture.

"Your name, madam?"

"Jennifer Wortham." The guard nodded and disappeared into an inner office. Moments later, a Vatican staff person appeared with a white envelope in hand, handing it to her. Jennifer opened it and pulled out a card with a Papal seal with a date on it. There was nothing else in the envelope.

"Um, where do we go?"

The Vatican staffer turned to the guard, who handed the staffer another sheet of paper with instructions, who then gave it to Jennifer. Jennifer quickly scanned the piece of paper and carefully folded it and tucked it away in her purse. "Thank you."

Back outside in the plaza, Jennifer and Michael decided to visit Saint Peter's Basilica. They walked quietly through the square decorated with fountains and an Egyptian obelisk that was transported to Rome in 37 AD. They entered the Basilica and were instantly overwhelmed by its beauty and reverence. They went in their own directions, each with their own thoughts.

Jennifer stood in awe, reflecting on the historical significance of the building, which is believed to have been built on the grave of Saint Peter. The great Church was decorated with large monuments, many of which were created by Gian Lorenzo Bernini, one of the greatest artists of all time. There were small chaplets sprinkled throughout the building, and statues of saints, and crucifixes and frescoes. It was breathtaking. Jennifer made the sign of the cross, said a silent prayer for the Church, and prayed for her family's healing.

After departing the Basilica, they walked down the street and visited one of the shops. A salesperson approached Jennifer. "Is there anything that you are looking for, Miss?"

With a nod, Jennifer replied, "A Saint Christopher medal."

The salesperson quickly stepped behind a glass counter and removed a velvet display tray with a variety of designs of Saint Christopher medals. "They're all so lovely," Jennifer remarked, and soon she had picked one out, paid for it, and had it wrapped in an exquisite little box. Then they perused the shop, finding a basement to the store that was filled with religious art and artifacts. Michael waited patiently as his sister spent time shopping, picking out several souvenirs for their nieces and all of her friends.

"Are we done shopping?" asked Michael in exasperation as they walked back out onto the busy street.

Jennifer said, "Only one thing left to do." She taunted Michael, and he rolled his eyes.

"What would that be?" he asked, fearing another shopping expedition.

"Pizza!" she yelled at him, and then added, "I'm famished."

Laughing joyfully, they walked around and found a quaint restaurant a few blocks down the street. Best of all, there were no lines. They sat at a window in the restaurant, watching people passing by and savoring the flavors of authentic Italian pizza as the cheese oozed over their hands.

"This is what heaven would be like for me," Michael said as he took another bite of pizza.

"Me, too," Jennifer concurred as she pulled a long string of cheese off her brother's face.

As they ate, Michael asked, "Are you ready for tomorrow?"

Jennifer contemplated the simple question, with its complex overtones. "Yes, I'm ready. Nervous, but..."

From their prior discussion in Venice, Michael knew how much this meeting with the Pope meant to her, and now he felt he had to support her. "Well, if you need to talk about it, let me know."

Jennifer reached for another slice of pizza and held it in the air. "After this, all I need is a hot bath and another glass of wine."

ENNIFER HAD A restful night thanks to the long hot bath and a second glass of wine. As she awoke, she stared at the ceiling. Daylight had just arrived and was filtering through the curtains. She rose from the squeaky bed and made her way to the window, squinting at the bright morning light and the Vatican in the distance. She believed God had called her here, and her heart was full and open. Whatever might happen, she committed herself to spend each day from this day forward to helping the Church in whatever way she could.

Jennifer put on a beautiful cream-colored lace dress, and bronze pumps. She styled her hair and put on earrings. She applied a light touch of mascara and dabbed some lipstick on her lips. When she was finished with her toiletry, she began to gather the things she would take with her on her visit to see the Pope.

She opened her backpack, unzipped the front pocket, and retrieved the little gold box with her grandmother's rosary and the Saint Christopher medal she had purchased the day before. She removed a folder from her backpack and sorted through the papers until she found the letter she had written to accompany the gift to the Pope. She reread it one more time:

December 28, 2016

Dear Holy Father,

Last spring, I was gardening in my backyard, and I discovered a lovely gift tucked neatly in a watering can surrounded by beautiful flowers. I showed it to my brother and my workers, and we all exclaimed that it was indeed a remarkable thing, a true gift from God. We debated what we should do with this gift, and we decided to leave it untouched in its place, hoping that its maker would soon return.

A few hours later, my worker called out my name and asked me to come back to the place we had found the gift. He showed me a container on the ground, and inside this container, nestled amongst the leaves and twigs, was another gift. Its inhabitants had long since departed, so I decided to bring this gift into my home to share with my family and friends, so they too might enjoy His beautiful creation. What a wonderful surprise it was to receive two such blessings from our Heavenly Father in one day.

I often visited the gift I left outside in the watering can to see if its maker had returned, but after several days I knew it had departed. So, I gently removed it from its vessel, and I brought it into my home so that it too could be enjoyed by others. For a time, these gifts rested in a bowl on the table in my living room. But this did not seem a fitting way for them to be displayed. My brother said we should craft these gifts into an art piece, and I struggled to find the best way to display them. In truth, they needed no other adornment, for they are perfect as He created them.

Several days later, I stumbled upon a beautiful set of petrified wood pedestals that appeared to be the perfect resting places for these unique gifts. I brought the pedestals home, and as I placed each gift upon them, I was surprised by the simple beauty of these treasures and the message they represented. I needed a name for these works of art, so I asked our Father his wish, and these words came me.

These gifts shall be known as His Love Springs Eternal. The pedestal, once a living thing, shall never turn to dust as all living things do. Rather, it shall endure and will serve as a testament to My creation for all time. The Gift upon the pedestal signifies that by My hand, all life is created, and through Me, all who have faith in Me will experience life eternal.

I prayed for guidance on what I should do with these treasures. They are true works of art by His hand, and surely they were meant for a place grander than my humble home. I was moved to give the first gift to a man who truly honors God in all that he does. He is pure of heart and generous of spirit; he serves as a living example of Christ and leads others to his path through his daily devotions in his work.

I am moved to present this second gift to you, your Holiness, for your good keeping in recognition of your great work in honor of the Jubilee of Mercy. He asks that you accept this gift in appreciation for all you have done to bring justice to those who have suffered, and for enlightening the world to the glory of Mercy.

Your humble servant,

Jennifer Susan Wortham

She put the letter back in the envelope and took from the backpack a little box containing some bars of wax and a seal with her initials that she had purchased in Venice. She dug into her purse and retrieved a box of matches, melted the end of one wax bar, and let it drip slowly onto the back of the envelope. She then stamped the wax to imprint her initials, and let it dry.

Jennifer next removed a piece of petrified wood from her suitcase and placed it in a brown box. She then retrieved the small box containing the bird's nest from her backpack, carefully unwrapped the nest, and placed it on the petrified wood. She then placed tissue over the petrified wood and put it all into the larger box. She closed the lid and tied it with string.

Grabbing her special pass, her purse, the items to be blessed, and her gift, she was ready to meet the Pope. Within minutes, Michael appeared at the door. He hugged her. All was ready, and they left. As they walked the few short blocks to the Vatican, Jennifer thought about how the trip had brought them even closer together.

Once they reached Saint Peter's Square, Jennifer's eyes grew wide, as she could not believe the thousands of people who were waiting to see the Pope. It wasn't clear where the line began and ended. "Oh my, I have no idea which way we should go!"

Men in uniform seemed to be available to answer questions, so Michael approached one and asked, "Excuse me, is this the line to see the Pope?"

The guide turned and looked at Jennifer, and then replied in a European accent, "Do you have a pass?" Jennifer nodded, and took out the envelope and removed the piece of paper written in Latin and showed it to the guard. "You should go to that line over there," he said politely as he pointed to the direction to the entrance.

They joined the designated line and waited their turn to enter. Almost to the door, Jennifer spotted a sign that read "No Packages Allowed." She felt a flutter of anxiety that they may not allow her to bring the package into the building. When they reached the entrance, she assumed the guards would question her package, so she immediately asked to speak with a supervisor. The Vatican Guard carefully inspected the package in her hands, called in other guards to stand by and watch the package, and then left. He returned shortly with a supervisor who also inspected her package with suspicion.

As they debated in Italian, Jennifer realized she should show them her pass. After reviewing the pass, the Guard Supervisor said, "Please open the box." Jennifer scurried to open the box. The Guard Supervisor took a long look inside. With pleading and desperate eyes, Jennifer urged, "It's a gift for the Pope."

The Supervisor of the Guards finally nodded his okay and gestured for the other guards to let her pass, pointing Jennifer to a door ahead. However, as Michael began to follow his sister, he was stopped by the Guard. "Only the person with the pass is allowed. You must go to that line and wait for the general reception."

Jennifer turned to Michael with downcast eyes. Her brother smiled and assured her that he would be fine.

"Go. I'll be okay."

Jennifer looked distressed, as she felt sick that her brother would not be able to join her. She almost turned back. But Michael shooed his sister with his hand. "Go, you better hurry." Jennifer smiled at her brother and said, "Thank you." Michael winked at her, and said more loudly, "Go" before turning around and heading back to the other line.

20

As JENNIFER ENTERED the Great Hall, alone, she felt badly that Michael was not able to be with her and said a silent prayer that he would find a way to get into the auditorium for the audience.

She soon saw a man in a distinguished-looking suit at the end of the hall, waiting at attention. When she arrived at his position, she handed him her pass, and he promptly escorted her to a row of seats at the very front of the Great Hall, seating her at the end of the row.

Jennifer took notice of the middle-aged man sitting next to her, a package tied in brown paper between them. He, too, has a gift for the Pope, she realized. After a moment, Jennifer engaged her neighbor in conversation. "Hello, my name is Jennifer," she offered.

The man nodded and said, "No English." Then Jennifer pointed to herself and said her name again. "Ah," said the man, and then he pointed to himself and said his name in Italian.

Jennifer didn't quite catch it, but she was too embarrassed to ask again, so she just smiled. Jennifer pulled her cell phone to search for the translation for "gift." Pointing to his package, she asked, "Regalo, Popa?"

The man smiled, "Si, si. Parla Italiano?"

She didn't understand, given his accent, that he was simply asking if she spoke Italian. She showed him her phone, with the translation.

He then said, "Ah, si. Piacere."

Jennifer looked up the words in her phone and replied, back in Italian, "Piacere di conoscerti troppo (Nice to meet you, too)," as they shook hands.

He showed her his package, saying, "Un libro."

Jennifer looked up the words in her phone, which translated to 'book.' Then she looked up a translation in response, "Sei l'autore?" and she gestured with her hands in a writing motion ('you are the author?').

He nodded. "Si, la mia signora." Once again looking at her translator, she found his response: yes, my lady. Then she looked up a reply.

"Che e meravig" (that is wonderful). Jennifer smiled as she struggled to pronounce the words.

A moment later the man beside her was then joined by another man. He said "Scusa, mia signora." That sentence needed no translation. Jennifer nodded, and the two gentlemen began conversing in Italian.

Jennifer turned around and tried to spot Michael, but

she couldn't see him in the large crowd gathering in the great auditorium. She sent Michael a text: "I can't see you. I am in the front row, to the left as you look at the stage. Where are you?"

"About twenty rows behind you. I'll wave to you," he texted back.

She stood up and looked toward the thousands of people behind her, and in the distance, she could see him waving. Jennifer was pleased that her brother had made his way into the hall. She waved back and texted him again: "I'm sorry you didn't get to come with me." Jennifer stared at her phone for his reply, which arrived a moment later. "It's okay. Do me a favor: ask the Pope to bless me."

"I will." Suddenly, a loud cheer filled the Great Hall as the Pope entered. As he moved down the center aisle, he shook hands with guests along the way. The Pope stopped to pray in front of a large picture of the Blessed Virgin Mary before seating himself in an oversized chair at the front of the altar. He made himself comfortable and looked out over the vast crowd of worshippers.

His eyes declared his love for them all, and he blessed them. Then he gave a brief sermon in Italian (which Jennifer could not understand, but his voice soothed her). There was a momentary pause, and then a completely unexpected thing happened. In came a strange display of entertainment: a circus act with jugglers and other attention-grabbing costumed characters in the tradition of the Commedia dell'Arte, the Italian Renaissance Theater.

The entertainment seemed a bit out of place in the Great Hall, but Jennifer noticed that the Pope appeared to be pleased and amused by it. Perhaps it was his way of bringing light to the tragedies of the world by reminding us that comedy and circus make us laugh and bring us joy.

When the entertainment was over, the Pope blessed everyone again, and the audience with him seemed to be over. Jennifer wondered what would happen next. Just then, the Pope made his way down the stage to the front of the rows of chairs.

He started at the other end of the row and blessed the sick and wedding couples, and then made his way down the line of chairs. Jennifer looked at the long row of people ahead of her and wondered if he would make it to her, or if would he depart before he got to her.

Out of nowhere, a Palace Assistant approached her. "Doctor Wortham?"

"Yes."

"His Holiness will greet you after the service. You speak Spanish?"

Jennifer shook her head. "No, only English."

"You have a gift for the Pope?"

Jennifer looked at the Palace Attendant with hopefulness. "Yes, it is here."

The Palace Attendant nodded again and then left Jennifer's side to speak with another gentleman. With each step that got the Pope closer to Jennifer, she felt more energized. It was as though there was a light glowing from inside her, and before she knew it, the Pope was standing in front of her. His Holiness seemed to know exactly who she was and why she was there as he took gentle hold of her hand.

The Pope looked at her directly, inquiring in a sweet Spanish accent, "Doctor Wortham, how was your journey?"

With reverence, Jennifer answered, "It's been quite an adventure, your Holiness. I am so pleased to meet with you."

The Pope looked deep into her eyes, and his eyes swelled a bit with tears. Jennifer was sure he was recalling what she had shared with him in her letter. "I am pleased you have made this journey. You have Christ in your heart, my child," the Pope softly expressed as he placed his hand on her head and said a blessing in Latin.

Jennifer felt an inner peace as never before, years of sadness dissipating in an instant. The Pope's sincerity and his humbleness touched her soul. She felt the depth of his faith, and she was awed by his immense spirit. His eyes had the innocence of a young child and the wisdom of an old soul at the same time. Then she knew: he would leave a lasting legacy on the Church.

The Pope did not walk away, as he had when shaking the hands of the others who were seated in the special section reserved for those who would meet him. He watched as she picked up the little box with the rosary and asked him to bless it for her. "Ah, yes; your grandmother's rosary." Jennifer nodded, amazed and pleased that he recalled that detail of her letter. He blessed it for her, and she felt at peace.

She then reached down to pick up her gift—the bird's nest resting gently on the petrified wood. Seeing it, the Pope smiled, his eyes lightened, and he became animated. He looked profoundly pleased with this gift, a simple, yet beautiful, creation of one of God's most treasured creatures. He realized the gift was more than a simple gesture of gratitude, as Jennifer shared that it signified Christ's eternal love for His people. It also signified a new beginning.

"What a wonderful treasure!" he beamed.

Jennifer explained her gift. "I found it in my backyard last April. This letter tells you about it and why I am giving it to you."

The Pope took Jennifer's hand again and placed his other hand over hers. "Thank you," he said softly.

There was a moment of silence, and the Pope and Jennifer seemed to be in a world of their own. Before he moved away, Jennifer asked him for one more thing. "My brother Michael is in the audience; would you bless him, your Holiness?"

She pointed in the direction of Michael in the audience, who was standing up, and the Pope waved to him, made a quick sign of the cross and uttered a blessing in his name.

Pope Francis took a step to depart from Jennifer, but then he turned back and looked deeply in her eyes. "You have Christ in your heart. Please pray for me."

Stunned by his unexpected request, Jennifer's eyes began to well up, and with conviction, she replied to him, "I will, your Holiness."

The Pope then left the Great Hall as though he was gliding

across the floor. Jennifer remained there in silence, exalted and immobilized by the experience. Never in her life had she experienced such a special moment of spiritual inspiration.

She stood in awe of the request the Pope had just made of her—to pray for him. As Jennifer reflected on this, a palace worker approached and handed her a card and a little packet with a rosary. She tucked it in her purse, then walked back in the direction she had entered.

When Jennifer exited the Great Hall, her brother was waiting for her, and they left the Vatican and walked into the plaza. Blue sky and sunshine welcomed them on a nippy December day. They felt blessed, literally and figuratively, and they walked around the Vatican grounds basking in God's glow and warmth.

21

LATER THAT DAY, the Pope returned to his private office
to rest and review some letters before moving on to his
evening engagements. A few of the gifts he received during the
general assembly sat on his desk. There was a book he received
from the Italian author, and then there was the bird's nest he
received from the doctor from America.

The Pope received hundreds of gifts each day; some lavish
ones from royalty, world leaders, and makers of luxury goods
seeking his blessings. By tradition, the most precious gifts
are given to the Vatican Museums, the Vatican Library, or the
Sacristy and Treasury Museum. But Francis decreed that usable
gifts be donated to charities. Other gifts are handled by the
Floreria Apostolica, an institution within the Vatican walls that
provides for furniture and decorations of the Holy Palaces and
for the setting of St. Peter's Square during the General Audiences.

The Floreria is full of hundreds of art pieces, sculptures, paintings, historical photographs, and signed books, each with their own story. But this was a first, he thought. What to do with a bird's nest? It sat on his desk, and he admired its intricate beauty. Then he picked up the package wrapped in brown paper. He opened it and removed a book from inside: it was about a homeless man. He began reading... But every now and then, his eyes flew across his desk to admire the little nest. The Pope enjoyed the simple things in life, and this was a gift to be treasured.

After the most peaceful night's sleep she had ever had, Jennifer and her brother returned to Vatican City the next day. The Vatican, also known as the Holy See, is a huge complex situated on a hill on the banks of the Tiber River. The city is made up of several palaces and connected buildings with over 1,000 rooms. Within the palaces are apartments, historic chapels, museums with art from every region of the world, special meeting rooms, and government offices, including the College of Cardinals, who serve as the Pope's cabinet.

Jennifer and Michael were again stunned by the enormous crowds, as each year millions of people travel to the Vatican to see the Pope, worship in St. Peter's Basilica, and appreciate the vast collections of art and relics held within the Vatican Museums. Much of the architecture, paintings, and sculpture that draw visitors to the city were created during the golden years of the Papal States and the great human Renaissance of the 16th century. Artists such as Michelangelo, Raphael, and Sandro Botticelli flocked to Rome to express their faith and dedication through the architecture and artwork of St. Peter's Basilica and the famed Sistine Chapel.

Jennifer turned to her brother as they stood in front of the Vatican entrance. "There are no words to describe how beautiful and holy this place is. I'm struck speechless," she continued.

"That's a first," Michael quipped with a laugh. He put his arm around her, and they entered the massive foyer of the Vatican. Mike purchased a guidebook and thumbed through it carefully as though he was looking for something. He stopped on the page with a picture of the Sistine Chapel, and his artistic soul poured out.

"When I was about 25, I came across the National Geographic magazine that featured the restoration of the Sistine Chapel. I had little exposure to fine art, other than the collection of art books at Grandma's house. I read the entire article and was astounded by the photographs of the restoration they did, especially the before and after photos comparing the ceiling blackened from years of candle and incense smoke. That was a pivotal moment for me. I bought my first set of professional art pencils and a large sketchbook, and I practiced drawing by copying Michelangelo's work. I had one of my drawings framed and hung it up in my apartment. Do you remember?"

"I do," said Jennifer. "It was really cool."

"It's what inspired me to pursue my degree in art," said Michael. They walked through the museum as Michael spoke of the various artists he had studied in art school, pointing out specific paintings he had copied in his Fine Art courses.

In the Sistine Chapel, Michael stared at the ceiling with awe. Jennifer was pleased to see Michael so at peace. He had beaten cancer after several years of treatment, but it had taken a toll on him. He was told that he would not survive, but he'd fought it hard. She was about to hug him when he pointed up at the famous portion of the ceiling where God reaches out to touch Adam's hand.

He whispered softly, "Michelangelo knew a lot about human anatomy. That's why his figures tend to have such huge thighs, with over-exaggerated muscles. But the real secret is that if you look closely at the area of Heaven where God is breaking through, it's shaped like a brain. Look, can you see it?"

Jennifer studied the area of the ceiling he was pointing at. "Wow, yes, I see it. I would never have noticed that!" Michael stood for a few moments, gathering his thoughts. "I think Michelangelo was telling us that God inhabits our minds."

Jennifer nodded at his statement. "That's a very interesting perspective."

He paused, lowering his eyes to meet hers, and said quietly, "I love his work: it's intimidating and inspiring at the same time." As they walked through the Chapel, Mike pointed out that Michelangelo had taken his revenge out on people he didn't like by painting their likenesses in or near Hell.

"I wouldn't have wanted to get on his bad side," Mike quipped.

"Me neither." The two siblings spent the next several hours viewing the immense collection of frescos, tapestries, jewels, antiquities, statues, paintings, and photographs in the Vatican's museums—the largest collection of art in the world. Timeless treasures had been collected together over the centuries, one by one, they had been woven into an artwork that made the Vatican one of its own. It was one of the greatest collections of man's accomplishments in the world.

As Jennifer walked along the corridors, her feet traced the steps of some of the world's richest, most famous and powerful people in history, yet all around her were crowds of average people of different faiths, races, creeds, colors, and vocations. The farmer, the banker, the lawyer, the doctor, the celebrity, mothers, fathers, sons, daughters, teachers, poets, rich and poor—all marveled together at the grandeur before them.

The Vatican's palaces had been built by the most skilled architects and craftsman of their time. Every inch of every wall, every inch of every floor, and every inch of every ceiling was painted by a master artist or adorned with precious stone, granite, and marble inlaid with rare gems and gold leaf gently laid by skilled masons. The sheer artistry and scale of their workmanship left her breathless.

In every room, there were frescos of angels, saints, and visions of Christ painted with precious minerals and rare pigments. Some of the angels in the paintings appeared as though they were in flight. When she closed her eyes,

Jennifer felt as though she was standing for a moment in heaven, the angels dancing around her to the most beautiful music she had ever heard.

Even the hallways that connected the rooms within the palaces had enormous tapestries from ceiling to floor, woven by hand in the finest silks of brilliant color; some taking decades to complete. There were murals, fountains, and marble statues carved by master artisans whose toiled-upon works created such glorious figures that one would believe they might come to life before their eyes.

The Vatican made Jennifer want to weep with joy, grateful to be alive, yet humbled at the same time. She thought to herself, who am I to be standing in the presence of such greatness? Then, she realized that these works were inspired by the greatest master of all, God, who bestowed the gift of creative vision and talent to the artists, craftsman, and stone workers. His vision became their vision so that we all might have a glimpse of the world as He wishes it to be, she thought. God wanted us to know the glory of heaven that awaits us through His eternal salvation. God, in His infinite wisdom, gave us these gifts to have and to hold. He has made these amazing works available to all humankind, whether they be rich or poor, so that we may revel in His glory.

As Jennifer and Michael departed the Vatican, they took a walk around the square and took pictures to remember their journey together.

They stopped into a restaurant for pizza and a beer and then headed back to their hotel. Jennifer was happy but exhausted from the day-long excursion to the Vatican. She fell asleep within minutes of hitting her bed, grateful for the precious time she had in Rome and the opportunity to meet such an amazing man.

22

I T WAS DECEMBER 30, two days after the meeting with Pope Francis. Jennifer and Michael sat in a café inside Leonardo Da Vinci-Fiumicino Airport, awaiting her flight back to Los Angeles. Michael planned to stay a little longer to travel to other cities in Italy. They had spent the past two days sightseeing in Rome as much as they could, excitedly exploring this city of antiquities and monuments that attested to the human achievements of Western civilization. They visited great churches and prayed (at least, Jennifer did), and they sat in restaurants and savored delectable meals made with care and expertise.

The time change of the trip and its emotional swings showed on their faces, though Jennifer was still on a high. "I don't want to go," she sighed.

Michael took a sip of his Italian coffee. "I know. Italy is a magical place."

Jennifer placed her hand on her brother's hand. "I want you to know how happy I am that we could do this together."

Michael took solace in his sister's heartfelt sentiment. "It was a great birthday present, thank you. I do feel some hope for the future of the Church...and for my life, for that matter," he added.

Jennifer looked up at her brother with hope and determination in her eyes. "You have to be patient. It's going to take time for things to change. While the Pope is the head of the Church, it's like any institution: if the leaders of the Church don't support him, he will fail. I know, from my own experience leading transformations, that it isn't easy. You can't just make things go your way. It's a long and difficult process, but I believe Pope Francis can do it."

Michael thought about what his sister was saying, and he nodded, seeming to understand her position.

Jennifer said, "Pope Francis asked me to pray for him, and I will. But I will also pray for all the leaders of the Church; that they open their hearts, listen to the people, and learn from their mistakes. I hope with all my heart that the Church is successful."

"Me, too," said Michael. "I really do."

They sat in silence for a moment, reflecting on the specialness of this trip. Jennifer turned to her brother and offered him an apology. "I'm sorry you didn't get to meet the Pope," Jennifer said with sincerity. "I really hoped we could both meet him."

Michael smiled. "We'll just have to come again, and we can bring Patrick, Mom, and the girls."

Jennifer smiled back. "Great idea. Perhaps we can all meet him together. Let me work on it." She looked at her watch. "I better get going. Take lots of pictures for me."

They hugged tightly and separated, each heading their own way. Not surprisingly, they turned around at the exact same moment and waved one last time. "Ciao!" Jennifer said and blew him a kiss.

Waiting in line at the departure gate, Jennifer reflected on her journey, an experience far beyond what she'd ever imagined. The ticket agent scanned her boarding pass, and she took a final look at the Rome airport terminal. It all clicked in her mind, and she realized that she could move on, knowing that a heavy burden had been lifted. She turned to the ticket agent and thanked her. As Jennifer moved down the bridge walk, she was soon out of sight.

Her flight home was like her arrival, requiring Jennifer to pass through Dusseldorf. There, she boarded the Air Berlin flight, a much larger aircraft holding several hundred passengers. Unbeknownst to her, Gabe arrived at the gate, running late, as before. He smiled at the cute ticket agent, who smiled back at the handsome gentleman as he made his way down the jetway. Then she closed the door, as he was again one of the last passengers to board.

As the plane climbed, the deep blue skies served as Jennifer's canvas. She stared out the window, painting a picture of finality and resolution, along with new opportunities for her, as the aircraft made its way northwards across Europe on its long trajectory back to Los Angeles. Sitting many rows behind her, in another cabin of the plane, Gabe busily read a European foodie magazine to enhance his culinary expertise. Occasionally, he, too, took a moment to look out the window and daydream about new opportunities painted on the canvas of his blue sky.

Half a day later, they landed in Los Angeles, a world apart from Rome. As Jennifer descended the escalator to baggage claim, one might say she had an aura about her. She saw the world differently than the day she'd departed the same terminal, full of tears and sorrow. Reaching the baggage carousels, she watched them rotate around like an amusement park game, with people waiting to claim their prizes. Suddenly, someone from behind tapped her on the shoulder. She turned and was surprised beyond belief.

Gabe smiled. "I guess we were on the same flight home. How amazing, again!"

"Gabe!!!" Jennifer beamed in surprise. "How was Germany?" she asked as she gave him a hug.

"It was marvelous, but now I am sad. I miss my friends already. I didn't want to come back," he admitted. "And you? How was your trip?"

Jennifer smiled broadly. "I met the Pope."

A quick response emitted from Gabe's open mouth: "You got in? What was it like?"

Jennifer nodded four times before saying, "It was, well, unbelievable."

"I want to hear all about it," said Gabe.

"I can do one better. I have pictures," said Jennifer as she pulled out a stack of photos from her backpack.

Gabe was astonished. "Wow, he actually shook your hand?"

"Yep. I received a blessing, and he blessed my grandmother's rosary," Jennifer said fondly remembering the special moment."

"What's this picture of?" asked Gabe.

"It's a bird's nest. It was my gift to the Pope."

"For real, you took a bird's nest to Rome!" Gabe exclaimed.

Jennifer nodded. "I did."

"It's beautiful. Tell me, where did it come from?" asked Gabe.

"I found it last spring when I was working in my garden. Then one day, I was taking a rest, and I had a vision that I was handing the nest to the Pope. That's why I wrote to him. I knew I was supposed to give the nest to him."

"That's unreal," Gabe said. Then he looked up as people began to swarm around the baggage carousel. "It looks like our luggage has finally arrived."

Jennifer and Gabe grabbed their bags and headed for the exit. The blast of cool December fresh air was a relief from the stifling terminal filled with people.

"I've got to get an Uber to get to Westwood, but I want to hear more about your visit with the Pope. Perhaps we can meet for lunch sometime soon?" asked Gabe.

"Why don't I give you a lift? I have my car," Jennifer offered.

"Are you sure? I don't want to inconvenience you," Gabe said a bit sheepishly.

Jennifer said, "It's no inconvenience. I don't have any plans, and it's on my way home."

Once in Jennifer's car, Gabe was dying to ask: "I don't want to intrude, but have you any news from Stephen?"

Jennifer kept her eye on the busy road ahead, but she smiled. "He called me on Christmas Eve. We've been texting, and we are going to talk. I have no idea what will happen, but I'm hopeful."

"That's great news," said Gabe.

"It never would have happened without you, Gabe. Thank you so much for your wise counsel."

Gabe's phone alarm suddenly rang. "Sorry, it's just about midnight in Germany. My friends are all together, and I want to call them."

"Why don't you Skype them?"

"Great idea. "Gabe quickly moved his fingers on his iPad, and within moments, the happy, cheerful faces of his friends were on the screen. "Happy New Year, Gabe! You are missing a great party," someone yelled out.

"Have a beer on me. Wish I was there!" Gabe said wistfully. They chatted about their day and wished each other good tidings. Gabe clicked off the screen and looked at Jennifer. "It's amazing how we can connect with our friends 2,000 miles away. The way technology is going, someday we will just be able to beam wherever we want to go."

Jennifer laughed. "I think that beaming up is a decidedly Christian phenomenon."

Gabe said, "You never know." Then he turned up the volume on the radio. The song playing was, "I'm Dreaming of a White Christmas." It seemed out of place on the sunny southern California day.

Being sensitive to Gabe's Jewish roots, Jennifer said, "Let's listen to some Beach Boys?"

"Great idea," Gabe said as he turned the station to a Beach Boys channel. They sailed down the 405 as 'Fun, Fun, Fun' played on the radio, and at the same time they both sang the lyrics 'Til her daddy takes the t-bird away,' and before they knew it, they'd arrived at their destination.

Jennifer put the car in park and turned to Gabe. "Here we are!"

Gabe thanked her and added, "Please, let's keep in touch."

Jennifer smiled. "I'd like that. Thanks again, Gabe, for everything." She gave Gabe a hug, and he got out of the car, grabbed his bag, and rolled away.

When Jennifer returned home, she called Stephen, and they decided to give their relationship another try. Whether it would work out in the end or not was unknown. But Jennifer had a new sense of what she wanted to accomplish in life—becoming part of a vast effort to help victims of child abuse and their families make peace with the Church

23

A FEW WEEKS after returning from Rome, Jennifer met her brother Patrick for lunch at the medical center where he works on weekends. After going through the cafeteria line, they headed out to an expansive outdoor patio filled with doctors in white coats, nurses in scrubs, and crowds of visitors enjoying a bit of respite in their otherwise busy day. The patio was full, as all wanted to be outdoors to enjoy the beautiful day. They held tightly onto their food trays, making their way through the maze of people and searching for an empty table. They found a pleasant spot by a fountain where the gentle flow of water provided a soothing backdrop.

A man in scrubs and a white coat stopped by as they were about to take their seats, and he asked, "Hi, Pat, how are you?"

Patrick gave the man a smile and replied, "I'm good, Dr. James. Have you met my sister, Doctor Wortham?"

The man looked at Jennifer and offered a pleasantry. "Nice to meet you. Pat talks about you all the time."

The doctor's pager buzzed. "Wish I could stay and chat. Got to get back to the E.R. It's a full moon, and it's been crazy today." The doctor departed, leaving the siblings alone to eat.

Patrick immediately asked Jennifer, as he took his first bites, "So, you got to see the Pope? Was it what you thought it would be?"

Jennifer smiled as she reminisced. "Yes. It was amazing. I'm sorry you couldn't come with us. I brought you some pictures." She scooted closer to Patrick and took out a huge stack of photos from her purse.

Patrick studied the pictures as Jennifer laid them out one by one on the table, narrating her journey. When she got to the photos of her and the Pope in the Great Hall, she looked at Patrick closely and said, "I wish you could meet him. He's a good man, Patrick. I could truly see it in his eyes."

Patrick took a deep breath, then a serious look appeared on his face as he nodded. "He is the only one in the Church who apologized about what they did."

Jennifer simply said, "I know." They sat in silence for a moment, no other words needing to be said.

Jennifer watched Patrick as he continued to look at the pictures. His particularly liked the photos of Venice. "I heard it's a really beautiful place."

Jennifer smiled in agreement. "It's magical. I'll take you there one day."

When Patrick was done going through the photos, he turned to his sister and asked about his daughters, who were living with her while their mother searched for an apartment. "How are the girls doing?"

Softly, Jennifer replied, "They are doing okay. They want you and their mom to get back together."

Patrick turned to Jennifer, and she could see the sweetness and innocence about her brother. Tears welled up in his eyes, and he quickly wiped them away. "That's what I want more than anything in the world, but I don't think she's going to come back."

Jennifer put her hand on his to comfort him and let him know how she had tried to help. "I had hoped that if I let her stay with me and we gave her time to reflect, things might work out." Patrick replied quickly, "It never works out for me."

Jennifer attempted to move the conversation in a more positive direction. "That's not true. You had some good years together, and you have two beautiful girls to be thankful for."

Silence set in as Patrick struggled to collect himself, tears threatening to fall from his eyes. "I don't want to lose my girls," he said as his grief mounted on his face.

"Patrick, that's not going to happen. You are a great father. Just because things aren't working out for you and their mom, doesn't mean you will lose your family."

Patrick picked up the photos and returned to glancing through them again, the pain of the conversation too much to bear. Finally, he said, "I feel like such a loser…" But then he immediately closed off his emotions as he abruptly handed the pictures back to Jennifer.

Jennifer turned to him and squeezed his hands. "You are a good man, Patrick, and a good provider for your family. You will find someone to love again; someone who will love you as you deserve to be loved."

Patrick stood up. "I have to get back to work."

Jennifer gathered her things as she got up to depart. Patrick gave Jennifer a quick hug, and then he was gone. In her heart, all she could think about was how she hoped that one day Patrick would find the happiness he deserved.

24

JENNIFER STIRRED HER cup of green tea and added a drop of honey. The aromas wafted up, and she saw out the restaurant window a woman with strawberry blond hair dressed in blue jeans, a long-sleeve tee, and a vest, crossing the street toward her.

They greeted each other warmly. "Hello, Doctor," said the woman, intentionally emphasizing the title.

"Patti, it's so good to see you," Jennifer replied, hugging this woman she had just started getting to know.

They ordered scones and a drink for Patti and chatted a moment until the food arrived.

"So how was Rome?" Patti finally asked excitedly. "You got to see the Pope?"

"Rome was beautiful, and yes, I got to see the Pope!" Jennifer said as she smiled broadly. Jennifer filled Patti in on her journey and the magical moments she had spent with Pope Francis.

"This is a fascinating story, Dr. Wortham, and the fact that you were able to capture the Pope's attention is very impressive. Someday, you're going to have to share that letter with me," teased Patti.

Patti admired Jennifer's courage in working through what must have been a very difficult situation for her. "In all those 'one out of million' chances, you found a way to his door," she said, shaking her head at the mystery of Jennifer's success in being invited to meet the Pope. After chatting some more and finishing her scone, Patti declared, "I want to put you on my TV show. I'd like to interview you about your visit with the Pope. What do you think?"

Jennifer didn't need to think much about Patti's kind offer. "I'd like that. I think it might help others to share my encounter with the Pope." Patti told Jennifer that she would set it up for as soon as possible. And, being who she was, within days, Patti got it filmed and done.

A few weeks later, Jennifer was checking her emails and found a note from Patti. It read:

Hi there,

Here is a link to the interview we did on the Pope:

https://tinyurl.com/interviewPope

You did a good job.

—Patti

The link led to Patti's 29-minute interview that she would soon air for her show, Intelligent Conversation, on KVET TV in the Palm Desert region of California. Jennifer clicked on it and watched. It opened with an image of hands filling the screen as Patti narrated what the audience was viewing.

"Those hands you see are the hands of a very nice lady, and the other set of hands that you see belong to none other, than... the Pope!" The image dissolved, and soon the audience watched Patti and Jennifer, sitting across from each other, reviewing the trip to meet Pope Francis and its significant implications for Jennifer.

"I read the letter you wrote...four or five pages long..." Patti said with admiration in her voice.

"Six pages," Jennifer interrupted playfully as they both laughed.

"Yes, six pages about why you wanted to meet him and what you thought of him," Patti continued, in genuine awe of the meeting.

Later in the interview, Patti held an object in her hand as Jennifer talked. Patti shared a thought: "I'm impressed with spirituality; and by spirituality, I mean all those who embrace a belief in something greater than themselves." Jennifer agreed, and the two women had a meeting of the minds as they spoke about the value of any religion in people's lives—how it uplifts you and provides a solid foundation for life.

Patti then lifted into camera view the item that occupied her hands, revealing Jennifer's grandmother's rosary.

A wide smile appeared on Patti's face, and the wonder in her eyes showed her excitement to be holding it. As a journalist, Patti had seen many things and met numerous people in her career, over the years, but it was this simple rosary, and the person sitting across from her, that made her eyes sparkle.

Jennifer spoke of how she had made it by hand when her grandmother was in her last days in a hospice. "It was apparent that she was finally at peace, and that was a reassuring feeling for me."

Jennifer then shared how much her grandmother was afraid of dying with so much unresolved in her life. "Dying is such a definite reality, but still very difficult to understand and manage," she noted. Jennifer fondly recalled her marvelous grandmother, to whom she had been so close, and who had led her to God through her own saintly life. Jennifer revealed that her grandmother had passed away with the rosary in her hand and her loving family by her side.

The interview then explored various aspects of Jennifer's life and what her spirituality meant to her. Jennifer explained to Patti, "The Catholic Church is my home. Its traditions serve as a tether that links me to Christ through the apostles, the priests, and those who have followed Him since his birth. I forgive the Church for its treatment of my family, and that is something I must personally do for my faith. But I do not excuse anyone in the Church who has abused a child, or those who perpetuated the cover-up of the many sexual abuse scandals. The abuse, the lack of oversight, and the general disdain for victims and their families once exhibited by church officials are inexcusable, and those responsible must be held fully accountable to the law of the land."

Patti probed about Jennifer's views on the Church and what this Pope who led the Catholic Church today could accomplish. The two women agreed on another point— that any discussions about the Catholic Church can be difficult and hurtful, especially given the fact that Jennifer's two brothers had been abused by a priest well-known to the family. As the interview continued, Jennifer and Patti found they shared many similar feelings about all organized religions and their role for humanity. They were in unison on the point that people should be allowed to live their lives as they wish and practice any religion they choose; but most importantly, they had to be good to one another and treat each other with respect.

The conversation between Jennifer and Patti then moved on to how this Pope appeared so different than previous Popes. Jennifer characterized him as a "servant of the people" in the warm, engaging style of leadership she had read about in the book called The Servant. In her view, Pope Francis sought to be one of the people, not accepting the perks of his office such as a grand residence and a chauffeured car. Instead, he lived a simple life, devoted to helping the poor and disadvantaged at any chance he could get. Jennifer noted, "This is a simple story about the true essence of leadership: to serve those who follow you."

As the interview wrapped up, Patti joked that anyone who might want to meet the Pope should have Jennifer write a letter for them.

25

GABE WAS WAITING patiently in the lobby of a lovely restaurant in Brentwood when Jennifer arrived and greeted him with a big hug. "Gabe, I'm so happy to see you." She was really looking forward to seeing him. He was so wise for his age; and genuine, and kind. One couldn't have a better friend.

Gabe stepped back and looked at his new friend. "Ditto. How are you?" They made their way into the restaurant, renewing their serendipitous treasured friendship as they were seated and served. As they ate a hearty breakfast, the two caught up.

"You seem very happy," Gabe said with a big smile on his face and joy in his eyes.

"I am," Jennifer replied.

Gabe took a long sip of his coffee as the server arrived and offered a refill. "So, you let go of your plans to be a nun?" he teased.

Jennifer nodded. "I believe God sent you to me to help me find my way." Jennifer's tone turned serious, and Gabe sensed that she was speaking from her heart. "Christ's gift to the world was to teach us to forgive one another, and to appreciate the blessings we receive from one other every day. I feel blessed to have met you, Gabe."

Gabe smiled, though he was a bit embarrassed, and asked, "So, what's next for you?"

Jennifer shared her plans. "I'm working on a book about forgiveness and my experience of returning to the church."

Gabe exclaimed, "That's great. I hope I can have a signed copy."

"Of course, you are one of the key characters," Jennifer said.

Gabe said, "Really? I never expected to be a character in a book."

"You are very important to me, Gabe: you were my Christmas gift from God," she said as she winked at Gabe mischievously.

Gabe laughed. "That's one for the record books: a Jewish, Buddhist, American, Israeli, average-looking guy you met on a plane was your Christmas Gift from God?"

Gabe's humor at the situation was contagious, and Jennifer couldn't stop laughing. When she finally composed herself, she said, "God sends us gifts every day. You just happened to arrive on Christmas."

"Well, I'm glad one of us got a Christmas present. Perhaps I'll get one next year," Gabe commented.

Jennifer's tone became more serious, "One never knows what God has planned for us."

Jennifer and Gabe spent the morning chatting about their work, their families, and their dreams for the future as the waitress returned several times to refresh their beverages.

Gabe shared with Jennifer that he was launching a new pastry business. Then he looked at his watch and said, "Wow, time flies. I have to run. I'm on the noon shift."

Gabe's Uber ride arrived, and they said their goodbyes and vowed to remain in contact with each other. As Gabe was getting into the car, Jennifer yelled out, "I'll pray for you, my friend."

The driver drove off, and Jennifer headed back to her car. Gabe always gave her something to think about.

26

WEEKS AFTER HER breakfast with Gabe, Jennifer sat in her office in Palm Springs. The first weeks of spring had all the desert flowers in bloom.

She sat at her computer and began to write a letter to the Pope to thank him for her visit, and to ask him for a special favor.

March 8, 2017

His Holiness, Pope Francis

Apostolic Palace

00120 Vatican City

Most Holy Father,

I wish to thank you for the opportunity to meet you and receive your blessing during my visit to Rome this past December 28th.

I have several treasured photos from my meeting with you, including the one enclosed. I have shared the photos and news of my joyous experience with my colleagues, friends, and family. You should know that in my daily travels, people of all faiths and nationalities comment to me that you are making a true difference in the world.

One colleague of mine, who is of the Jewish faith, said: "I love this Pope. I'm not Catholic, but I feel as though he is my Pope." You inspire us to be better people, your Holiness, and you have truly enlightened many to the blessing of Mercy.

As I shared in my last letter to you, I desire to help others discover the grace of Mercy and the blessings of forgiveness that is the legacy of our Lord Jesus Christ. I believe it is my duty to share the peace and joy I experienced through committing my heart and soul to His service. I am writing to ask you a favor, but first I wish to share another piece of my journey with you to provide the context for my request.

When I was 15 years old, my mother and stepfather and I took a summer outing to Disneyland. My stepfather suffered a massive heart attack at the park, and he passed that afternoon. He was just 40 years old. His passing devastated my mother, and she was inconsolable for several months. Her health suffered, and it was difficult for her to work and to make ends meet. So, I went to work as a nurse aid at a local hospital, and I took on many of the responsibilities of caring for the family.

My brother Patrick was 13 years old at the time, and following our stepfather's passing, he became quite angry with the world. He had several run-ins with the law, and he was failing in school. I didn't understand why he was so angry.

I took it upon myself to find a solution to the havoc my brother was creating for my mother. I reached out to Father Howard for help. He was the priest I spoke of in my last letter. I hoped that he would be able to assist me with my brother and provide relief for my mother, as he had been so close to my family during his time serving our parish.

As you know, it was many years later that I learned of Patrick's abuse at the hands of this priest. Patrick once shared with me that he was angry because he believed at the time that God took our stepfather to punish him for "being" with a priest. Of course, he was much too young to have any blame for these incidents.

Father Howard was serving as a pastor in a parish in Texas when I called him. I explained what was happening, and he invited Patrick to come to stay with him at the rectory for the summer. My grandparents purchased a plane ticket, and we made the arrangements. As the time neared for Patrick to depart, he begged us not to send him. I'll never forget him screaming, "Please don't make me go; please, Jenny, I promise I'll be good." I did not know that Father Howard had molested my brothers during his time in our parish, so I ignored his pleas, hoping against hope that Father would work a miracle and help Patrick through his grief.

When Patrick returned home a few months later, he was very depressed. He internalized his rage and became withdrawn. He turned to drugs to ease his suffering. He has struggled with the shame of his childhood abuse since that time, and last year he lost his marriage as a result.

Patrick works two jobs to provide for his family. He is honest and kind to others. He has a good soul. He believes in God, and he is an honorable man.

I have long carried a great deal of guilt for failing Patrick during his time of need. Although I was just a young girl at the time, trying to help my mother, my actions in sending him to live with the priest changed his life forever. While I have forgiven the priest, and the church, it was much harder for me to forgive myself.

I wish to find a way to help Patrick and others like him to find peace. I have prayed on the matter for many months, and I believe the Holy Spirit has answered my prayers in providing me with a vision to create a special day for reconciliation for those who have suffered abuse as children.

You have publicly acknowledged the Church's past transgressions, and you have taken great measures to protect children from harm. I am aware that the Church has funded counseling and supportive services to help children and their families recover. However, there are still places in the world where children are abused, sold into slavery, and used in the vilest of manners. These transgressions in our society must be stopped. I wish with all my heart for your support in establishing this day of reconciliation to raise awareness and funding to help those who are suffering.

Patrick's birthday is April 8th. It would be a great honor to Patrick, and those like him who are suffering, if you would dedicate a special Mass and declare April 8, each year, from this year forward, a day of reconciliation for victims of abuse.

On this day, I would ask people of all faiths, from all nations, to pray for the children who have been victimized by those entrusted to care for them. I would begin a petition to governments the world over to take action to end child marriages, prevent the trafficking of children, and to help end violence against them. Finally, I would ask for all the priests in our church to pray that the Holy Spirit touches the hearts of these victims, so that they may forgive those who have transgressed against them, and finally, find peace.

I am sending you 60 beautiful handcrafted ribbons for those in your service who wish to wear them on April 8th, in honor of my request. The blue ribbon is often used as a symbol to raise awareness of child abuse. The white ribbon shall serve as a beacon of His mercy. Together, these ribbons shall serve as a covenant against child abuse that will inspire action, bringing a measure of solace to these victims and their families.

If you grant my request, I wish to bring my family to Rome to celebrate this mass with you in hopes that it will help my brothers and my mother heal, so that they too may finally make peace with the Church.

I am most grateful for your consideration of my request. You are always in my thoughts and prayers, your Holiness.

Your most humble servant,

Jennifer Wortham

Jennifer cried as she finished her letter. The years of pain and grief washed over her as she recalled her own actions that had so impacted her brother's life. She closed her eyes for a moment to pray, and then she printed the letter and shut off the laptop, confident that her letter was complete and ready to send the Pope.

A few days later, Jennifer picked up the ribbons from the seamstress who had graciously offered to make them for this important occasion. She placed a pin on each of the ribbons so that they could be attached to the Bishops vestments. She placed the ribbons in a white box with tissue, then placed the letter on top of the box and wrapped the box with a blue and white ribbon and pinned the ribbon with a large golden cross. She wrapped the package in brown paper and tied it with string. Later that day, Jennifer took the package to the Federal Express office and had it shipped.

As she walked out of the Federal Express building, she felt as though a huge weight had been lifted from her shoulders. It had been a very long journey to forgiveness, for herself and the Church.

27

JENNIFER TOOK A break from a busy schedule to lunch with her mother at their favorite place, Martha Green's The Eating Room. It was autumn, and the bakery was loaded with homemade pumpkin pies and apple fritters. The sweet smell of nutmeg and cinnamon greeted her as she walked into the dining room, the warm spices immediately bringing back memories of the wonderful times spent with her grandmother, baking cookies and pies for the holidays.

Judy called to say she was running late, so Jennifer ordered a cup of hot tea and took out her computer to catch up on her emails. When Judy arrived, her hair was tousled and blown from the wind of an unusually blustery fall day. She leaned over and kissed her daughter on the cheek. Once her mom got settled, Jennifer asked, "How are you?"

Judy beamed and declared with enthusiasm, "I'm wonderful. I really like retired life."

Jennifer saw how happy her mom was. "Retirement looks good on you."

"I'm getting used to sleeping in late and taking long naps," said Judy.

Dorothy arrived, as always, and the ladies ordered their usual lunch. Waiting for their food, they began talking about their plans for the coming holidays. Judy asked her daughter, "How are things with you and Stephen?" Jennifer was silent for a few minutes while they ate their lunch. Judy noticed a shadow cross her daughter's eyes. "Is everything okay?"

Jennifer reflected for a minute, not sure what to say. "You know, Mom, all relationships have their ups and downs," she said in a voice more serious than before. "Whatever happens in life, I've come to realize that the only constant we have is God."

Judy smiled, knowing that her daughter's faith would get her through anything life threw at her. Changing the subject, she asked, "How is your book coming along?"

"It's taking a lot more time than I thought. I did finally receive a response to my last letter to Pope Francis, though!"

"Tell me," Judy said, getting excited.

"See for yourself. I made you a copy," Jennifer said, pulling an envelope from her purse.

Secretariat of State

From the Vatican, 30 October 2017

Dear Dr. Wortham,

The Holy Father has received your letter, and he has asked me to reply in his name. He appreciates the concern which prompted you to write to him.

His Holiness has remembered your brother Patrick in his prayers, and he invokes upon you God's blessings of strength and peace.

Yours sincerely,

Monsignor Paolo Borgia —Assessor

Judy glanced over the letter on its simple stationery. She sensed her daughter's disappointment. "Well, honey, he didn't actually say no to your request for a day of prayer. Perhaps he's thinking it over," Judy said with a hint of encouragement in her voice.

Jennifer wasn't so sure. She had a definite downcast look, and said to her mother, "Who knows if he even got my letter? He gets thousands of them every day, far more important than mine. I was lucky the first one made it through to him."

Judy folded the letter and placed it in her purse. "Have a little faith; you never know what might happen," she said.

Jennifer recalled that she had one more thing to share with her mom. She reached into her briefcase and took out a book. "I just read this wonderful book that Pope Francis wrote, called

The Joy of Love. I bought you a copy," Jennifer said as she handed the book wrapped in pink tissue paper to her mother.

Judy opened the book with delight and exclaimed, "I'm going to have to buy a new bookshelf for all of these books you bring me!" Jennifer laughed.

Jennifer reached for the book and flipped through its pages to find a passage. "You have to read this, Mom.

"This specific chapter has raised a lot of eyebrows in the Church because Pope Francis advises priests that they should be open to working with 'imperfect couples' to help them reconcile to their faith. For instance, he wrote that priests may consider granting the Sacrament of Marriage to Catholics who married in the Church, and have divorced and remarried in civil ceremonies without an annulment. He also advised that priests may consider allowing these couples to accept communion."

Judy looked up with doubt. "Really?"

Jennifer continued, "It's a rather progressive concept for the Church, but the world is full of 'imperfect' Catholics." Jennifer thought about the many Catholics she knew who left the Church because they had married in the Church but then divorced and remarried outside of the Church, and many more who were unmarried and cohabitating. Most of these people gave up on the Church because they were not allowed to partake in the sacrament of communion. "I believe the Pope is offering an olive branch of sorts to disenfranchised Catholics, in hopes that they might find their way back to the Church."

Judy stared at her daughter, still trying to absorb the news she had just shared. "That's hard to believe. I can't see the Church changing that much."

Jennifer replied, "It true." Jennifer and her mother took a moment to reflect each in their own world of thoughts. Jennifer broke the silence. "The road ahead for the Pope will be rough. While he is more progressive than many forces in the Church are willing to accept, I do believe he will find a way to transform the Church while still holding true to the most meaningful, sacred Catholic traditions of honoring Christ and all that He taught us about love and forgiveness."

Dorothy arrived to clear their plates. "Will you ladies be having carrot cake, as usual?"

Jennifer looked at her mother with a mischievous glint in her eyes and said, "No, I think it's time for a change. How about some apple pie and vanilla ice cream?" Judy laughed.

"You got it: two apple pies, a la mode," Dorothy chuckled as she departed.

While the two ladies sat enjoying the fresh-baked apple pie, Judy could see the wheels turning in her daughter's head. "What's on your mind?"

"I've been praying about what I should do about the Vatican's response to my letter. I know it would mean a great deal to survivors like Patrick and Michael if the Pope would dedicate a special mass every year for those who have been abused. I believe a special mass at the Vatican dedicated to survivors, with the Bishops and Cardinals all present, would provide a sense of justice to survivors and their families. It would show us that we are truly cared for by the Church, and for some, it would bring healing and closure!"

"I agree with you, a Mass in honor of survivors would be a great gesture of goodwill," said Judy.

"Maybe I'll just fax the Vatican a copy of my manuscript..."

"You're going to break their fax machine," Judy teased.

Jennifer laughed out loud. "I'm not giving up. I'll figure out some way to convey my message to the Pope. Wow, time flies, I've got to get back to work, Mom.."

Judy smiled broadly at her daughter, her enthusiasm contagious. "Thank you for treating me to lunch, it was lovely."

"Of course Mom. Thanks again for always being there for me," Jennifer said as she hugged her mother.

Jennifer walked her mother to her car. Before getting in, Judy turned and kissed her daughter on the cheek. "You know, you would have made a fierce nun."

"You never know what God has planned for us," Jennifer said, and smiled, thinking of all that had happened in the past eighteen months.

Judy got into her car, then closed the door. Then she rolled down her window and shouted to her daughter, "A piece of advice, honey. Instead of spending all your free time writing letters to the Pope, next time you meet him, why don't you just ask him for his phone number?"

Jennifer laughed at the thought. "I may just do that."

APRIL 2, 2018. Judy read the manuscript her daughter had written. Turning the last pages, tears filled her eyes as she came to a deeper understanding of what her daughter was trying to accomplish. She picked up the phone and dialed Jennifer's cell.

"Hi Mom, how are you?" answered Jennifer.

"I'm fine. Guess what? I already finished reading your book!" exclaimed Judy.

"Wow that was fast. I just sent it to you a few days ago," Jennifer said.

"Well, it arrived yesterday and once I started reading it, I couldn't put it down. I was up until 1:00 a.m. I loved it. You did a great job and you should be proud of yourself," Judy praised.

"Thanks, Mom. I know that a lot of what I had to say will be controversial. However, I really believe in my mission to establish a Day of Healing for Survivors of Abuse."

"What can I do to help you?" Judy asked.

"I was hoping you'd be willing to write a letter to the Pope.

Could you do that? I could post it on my website and maybe it would encourage others to write, as well," Jennifer said.

Judy was quiet for a moment. "Let me give it some thought. When do you need the letter?"

Jennifer didn't want to pressure her mother. "No rush. Just write it whenever you feel the time is right. I think it is important for the Pope to hear what you have to say."

"Okay, dear, I'll work on it. Have a great day at work," Judy said.

Jennifer wished her mother a nice day as well. "And thanks, Mom. I knew I could count on you."

Judy reflected for several weeks on how she might fulfill her daughter's request. Jennifer's story had brought up a lot of feelings she thought had been laid to rest. It had been an emotional journey of highs and lows for her as she realized she had begun her own journey of forgiveness.

In the past several months, there had been many more reports of abuse by priests all around the world. It seemed like there was a new report every week. It broke her heart to read these stories and think about how the families, especially the mothers of these children, must be feeling to have their experiences made public for the entire world to see. She felt she needed to do something to help the situation, so she visited her local diocese and offered to work with the families of survivors. She now believed deeply in what her daughter was working to accomplish. She became convinced that her own letter to the Pope might help.

One evening after yet another report about a sexual abuse scandal in the Church had made headline news, she felt inspired to write. She sat at her desk and the words just began to flow. Within a few hours, Judy emailed the draft of her letter to her daughter with a quick note: "Dear Jennifer, I finished writing my letter to the Pope (attached). I hope this is helpful to your mission."

Jennifer opened her email the next morning and read her mother's letter as she sipped her cup of hot tea.

Dear Holy Father,

The sexual abuse of children by pedophile priests in the Catholic Church is a difficult topic to read about and live through. Cloaked in their own deep dark secret, the survivors suffer from the power and fear of authority used against them in a "Don't ever tell" shame that makes them feel it is their fault for having participated in an "intimate" act with their priest. This secret destroys the lives not only of the survivors but their families.

How is it possible that two children raised by a loving, nurturing extended family who provided religious training, excellent schools, Cub Scouts, Boy Scouts, Little League baseball, AYSO soccer, Little League football, figure skating, fishing, and who celebrated birthdays, holidays, and special occasions with family and friends, surrounding them with love and affection, and who had the bragging rights of polite, well-behaved, happy children with the oldest boy thriving in school as a straight "A" student who wanted to become a doctor—became a teen rebel in a world of gangs and drugs?

It was their secret that destroyed them, but it took many years for me to realize this.

One summer afternoon, our neighbor was asked to find my boys at the local movie theatre and bring them home due to a family emergency. Once home, they were greeted by the family and our parish priest and told that their stepfather had suffered a heart attack and died. He was only 40 years old. Looking back, I blamed this tragic life event as the cause of their gradual change in behavior. They refused to actively participate in counseling sessions, all the while hiding the true cause — their secret.

It was not until my sons were in their twenties that their secret was revealed to me, after years of agonizingly desperate attempts to get my oldest son into drug rehabilitation programs and counseling to try to save him. During his last crisis, I had all but given up when, out of the blue, his younger brother revealed their secret to me. Only then did I finally understand.

I felt such rage that my body trembled, and animal-like screams came from the depths of my soul. How could this be? How could this happen to my beautiful boys? How could our parish priest, a long-time family friend, betray our trust and faith? I felt so helpless, as though it was somehow my fault for not knowing, and felt like there was nothing I could do about it now, after so many years had gone by. It took years for me to be able to drive past a Catholic Church without trembling with hate and feeling nauseous.

Had this been one incident with one pedophile priest, I could have better reconciled it. But learning through publicized scandal after scandal that this was rampant behavior among hundreds of priests, as well as Church policy to transfer the pedophile priests to other parishes, made me realize that my family was only one in thousands victimized by these vile men who, once discovered, were simply transferred from parish to parish and never were reported by the Church for their criminal behavior. Over the past 25 years, I tried everything to help my sons heal, but to this day they still suffer from the wounds of their experience—wounds that reside deep within their souls.

While I had all but given up hope, I now have the honor and privilege of being the mother of a daughter who met you and reported back that you had kind eyes and she trusted you to be an agent of positive change in the Church. Jennifer felt touched by the Holy Spirit to help heal and nurture survivors suffering from sexual abuse and to seek your help to accomplish her mission. Jennifer shares her journey with you in the pages of this book. As you read her story, please know that she helped me heal and forgive the Church by reconnecting me in my devotion to our Blessed Virgin Mary.

I now find great comfort in visiting the Chaplet of Divine Mercy to pray, carrying the beautiful rosary my daughter presented to me this past Mother's Day, made by her own loving hands. Upon entering the Chapel, I first light a votive candle, as I was taught to do as a child by my devout and loving Mother, to offer devotion and prayer to our Blessed Virgin Mary. My fervent prayer is that my two sons will someday overcome their pain, and find peace in their hearts.

God bless my precious daughter for leading me back from the ashes to the grace of God through her selfless love and dedication to her faith.

I ask you to support Jennifer's vision for a Day of Justice and Healing, so that survivors of abuse the world over and their families may find their own path to forgiveness and peace with our Holy Mother Church.

Sincerely,

Judith Ann

Deeply touched by her mother's words, Jennifer picked up her cell phone and dialed. "Hi Mom, I hate to interrupt your breakfast with Dan, but I want to thank you for writing this beautiful letter; it's perfect. You did a great job, Mom, thank you so much," Jennifer commented.

"Well, I hope the Pope reads your book and understands how much it would mean to the thousands of survivors and families who have been impacted by child abuse to have a dedicated Day of Healing," Judy said.

Jennifer held back tears as she thought of all her mother had done to support her through this process. "Thanks, Mom, you have been such a great inspiration to me. I really appreciate your help with this letter and all your understanding during my reconciliation and your support of my book. I couldn't have done this without you."

Epilogue

WHILE I FORGAVE the Church for its actions against my family, I do not condone or excuse anyone who abuses a child, or protects an abuser from justice. Those who commit such crimes must be held accountable for their actions.

Many Catholics have responded to the reports of clergy sexual abuse with outrage and disgust. They want answers, and some have called for voluntary resignation of the leadership of the Church. But, such an action will not solve the problem of child sexual abuse. As I shared in the introduction, child sexual abuse is not just a problem for the Catholic Church to solve. It is a problem for society at large to solve.

The leaders of the Catholic Church are culpable for the culture they created, and they are responsible to ensure that those who have been victimized by their clergy have access to the resources they need to heal. Now that the reports of the extent of the cover-up have become public knowledge, the Church must finally come to terms with the problem and take whatever actions are necessary to restore the faith and goodwill of the people they serve.

We must not forget that there are tens of thousands of good priests, sisters, deacons, and lay leaders in the Church with strong convictions who practice their faith with grace and dignity in Christ's name. These good people tend to our spiritual needs, care for the sick, educate our youth, and provide significant social benefits for the poor and vulnerable people in our communities.

While many have criticized the Church for failing to adequately address the child abuse issue, in truth the Church has been working diligently over the past two decades to find a solution to this tragic situation.

On August 16th, 2018, the Vatican released the following statement regarding the Pennsylvania Grand Jury report:

"Most of the discussion in the Pennsylvania Grand Jury report concerns abuses before the early 2000s. By finding almost no cases after 2002, the Grand Jury's conclusions are consistent with previous studies showing that Catholic Church reforms in the United States drastically reduced the incidence of clergy child abuse. The Holy See encourages continued reform and vigilance at all levels of the Catholic Church, to help ensure the protection of minors and vulnerable adults from harm. The Holy See also wants to underscore the need to comply with the civil law, including mandatory child abuse reporting requirements. The Holy Father understands well how much these crimes can shake the faith and the spirt of believers and reiterates the call to make every effort to create a safe environment for minors and vulnerable adults in the Church and in all of society.

Victims should know that the Pope is on their side. Those who have suffered are his priority, and the Church wants to listen to them to root out this tragic horror that destroys the lives of the innocent."

On August 20, Pope Francis also issued a letter to Catholics around the world condemning the "crime" of priestly sexual abuse and its cover-up and demanded accountability, in response to new revelations in the United States of decades of misconduct by the Catholic Church.

"Let us beg forgiveness for our own sins and the sins of others," he wrote. "An awareness of sin helps us to acknowledge the errors, the crimes, and the wounds caused in the past and allows us, in the present, to be more open and committed along a journey of renewed conversion."

In a Mass at Dublin's Phoenix Park on August 26, 2018, Pope Francis again asked for forgiveness for what he called "abuses of power perpetrated by members with roles of responsibility in the Church."

"We ask forgiveness for some members of the Church's hierarchy who did not take charge of these painful situations and kept quiet," said Francis. The Pope met the prior day with victims of all sorts of abuses: sexual abuses and child labor, as well as children wrenched from their unwed mothers and forcibly put up for adoption.

These are good steps in the right direction, but there is much work to be done.

Through sharing my journey of healing and forgiveness of the Church with my Mother, she found her way back to the Church. This book is a testament of our journey. We hope that in some small way our journey will help others heal.

As a member of a family with two sex abuse victims, I have been reassured by the Pope's remorse, his commitment to protecting children and young people in the Church, and the actions he has taken to solve this problem. As a public health professional, the Pope's response to the Pennsylvania Grand Jury report intrigued me. Had the actions the Church has taken in the past two decades reduced the incidence of sexual abuse? If so, what might be learned from the actions and reforms the Church had instituted? How can these lessons be used to help end sexual abuse in other institutions, schools, and religious organizations? What can be done to help survivors and their families heal?

As a Catholic, I wanted to know what might be done to restore the faithful's confidence in the leaders of our Church.

These are questions that should have answers. Thus begins the next phase of my journey.

Following is the introduction to my next book. As my mother once told me: "Have faith; you never know what the future might bring."

I hope you enjoyed my story.

Faith in Forgiveness

Prologue

After several letters and multiple phone calls, I had finally obtained a meeting with Cardinal O'Malley, the President of the Pontifical Commission for the Protection of Minors. I had initially contacted the Cardinal's office to ask for his support for dedicating a day for justice and healing for survivors of abuse. In the days that led up to my meeting, however, I had an even more important mission. I wanted to learn all I could about the various programs, policies, and initiatives the Vatican had implemented to help decrease the incidence of clergy sexual abuse after learning that the number of abuse cases had declined precipitously in recent years.

The summer of 2018 had been brutal for the US Catholic Church, with reports of clergy sexual misconduct making daily headline news. However, none of the reports included the news of the changes the Church had made, nor did they report statistics, mention the decline in the abuse cases in the last two decades, or provide anything based in scientific fact. I wanted to find a way to help the church. The academic in me was interested in discovering what the Church had done that might help with this global public health problem.

I was invited to meet the Cardinal at the rectory of the Holy

Cross Cathedral. It was a short cab ride from my hotel, and the driver took pride in pointing out some of the historic points of interest along the way. I got out of the cab and walked up the steps of a quaint brownstone building located in the vibrant South End of Boston. The street was strangely quiet. I stood at the front door for a moment to calm myself, as I was a bit nervous. I had no idea of how I would be received by the Cardinal, or how my request might be viewed.

I took a moment to compose myself and rang the doorbell. A few minutes later a middle-aged priest wearing casual clerical clothing consisting of a black shirt with a white collar, and plain black dress slacks, opened the door.

"Hello, you must be Dr. Wortham," the priest said with a smile, the warmth of his greeting reaching his eyes. I nodded my head in the affirmative. "Please call me Jennifer," I said as I reached out and shook his hand.

"I'm Father Kickham, welcome to Holy Cross."

"Thank you, I'm so pleased to meet you," I said as I walked across the threshold.

Father Kickham escorted me to a small parlor with a little coffee table and four lounge chairs to await the arrival of the Cardinal. The rectory furnishings were simple, yet functional. A few minutes later, lights flickered in the room across from the parlor, and shortly thereafter Father Kickham came to escort me to the Cardinal.

We entered a small conference room with a long wooden table with about 20 chairs. The room was rather austere, except for a few prints of various religious scenes in simple wooden frames hanging on the wood paneled walls.

When I entered the room, I noticed the Cardinal was sitting

at the head of the table. He wore a plain brown tunic like the ones I had seen worn by of those of the Franciscan order. As I neared the head of the table, he stood and greeted me. He offered me coffee, but I declined. We had just 30 minutes for our meeting. I had a many things I wished to discuss, and I didn't want to waste a second of our time together.

The Cardinal shook my hand, but he appeared somewhat guarded. He sat down and looked at me with a bit of skepticism in his eyes. I realized he was assessing me, wondering if I was to be a friend or a foe. I understood his position and I attempted to put him at ease, smiling as I retrieved the list of questions I had prepared from my briefcase.

I shared a bit of my background and some of my family's story. Although he answered my questions politely, the Cardinal was fairly cordial, as though he was being interviewed by a member of the press.

I began, "Although the Pope has publicly acknowledged the abuses of the clergy, and he has apologized for the Church's response, he has not dedicated a day for recognition of the abuse. I believe the survivors and their families would benefit from the Church designating a day to help survivors begin healing from the spiritual wounds they have endured," I said.

The Cardinal listened intently, and finally responded. "The leadership of the Church has considered such a day, but it was determined that each Diocese should select a date that works best for their community. The Catholic Bishops held a Mass of prayer and penance last year at the opening of their conference, and the Boston Diocese held a special Mass to honor survivors. Several survivors shared their stories, and we all prayed together for the recovery of all those who had been harmed by the Church. It was quite moving."

The Cardinal sat back in his chair and listened intently as I responded. "That does sound quite inspiring. I had no idea. How are these Masses publicized?" I asked.

The Cardinal became a bit more animated. "We announce them at the end of Mass, and we list all of our special events in the Church bulletin and on our website."

"I see." I took a moment to think of a response that wouldn't offend the Cardinal. "I mean no disrespect, but for those victims and their families, and other disenfranchised Catholics who have left the Church, how are they to know about these events?"

Father Kickham spoke up: "We do work with the media and we send out press releases, but they don't always cover these events."

I couldn't help myself from pressing my point. "I ran a public relations firm for several years, and I understand that the media has many competing priorities. But, you know, I believe that if the Vatican dedicated a special day for prayer and reflection, and it was celebrated with a special Mass at each diocese on the same day, such an event might be highly publicized. It would mean a great deal to the survivors and their families to know the Church is praying for them. It would also heighten their awareness of the programs and services available to them, and I believe it would help improve the reputation of the Church." Then I remembered who I was addressing and added, "In my humble opinion, Your Eminence."

The Cardinal sat back again. I looked into his eyes, searching for some sign that he might understand. But years of experience in politics and dealing with the press had made him very adept at keeping his thoughts to himself. I realized that my request would not go any further at this point, so I pivoted to the other item on my list. "Thank you for considering my request. If you have a few more minutes to spare, I have one other item I wish to discuss." Cardinal nodded in affirmation that I could ask my question.

"As you are aware, I am working on a book detailing my family's experience with the Church. I recently heard Pope Francis's response to the Pennsylvania Grand Jury report, and something he said caught my attention." I sat quietly for a moment, gathering my thoughts. "Pope Francis said that the Church had done a great deal to protect minors from abuse, and that the incidence of clergy child sexual abuse had gone down significantly in the past two decades."

The Cardinal nodded. Then Father Kickham interjected: "Yes, it has declined. The Church instituted several programs and procedures to combat the problem after the crisis in Boston in the early 2000s. We have instituted a zero-tolerance and mandatory reporting policy. We conduct in-depth assessments of all men who are entering the seminary, and we do background checks on all staff. We are working very hard to ensure a safe environment for all children and youth in the Church."

"It sounds like you have accomplished a great deal. Thank you for sharing the information with me. I reviewed your website and did some research, and I was very surprised by what I learned. I would like to gain a better understanding of your work, and include a list of the policies and programs the Commission has implemented in my book. I will be traveling to Rome next month and I wondered if I might meet with your staff during my visit to become more acquainted with all of the initiatives you have underway."

The Cardinal agreed that I could visit with his staff, and Father Kickham offered to help me set up some meetings. He also gave me the names of several individuals and organizations they were working with to help survivors heal.

Although the Cardinal did not encourage me to pursue the Day of Justice and Healing. I still had hope. I was grateful for the time he and Father Kickham took to meet with me and I was encouraged that I might have the opportunity to meet with the staff of the Commission during my trip to Rome.

"Thank you so much for meeting with me. I know you have many pressing matters, and I am grateful that you made time for me." I stood up to depart, and shook the Cardinal's hand. Then Father Kickham showed me to the door.

The same driver who had brought me to the Cathedral was waiting for me where he had dropped me off. I was pleased, as I had a plane to catch, and I knew Sunday evenings at the busy international airport could be quite hectic.

As we glided down the freeway, I reflected on my meeting with the cardinal. I sensed he was weary from the near-constant media attention and political crisis the Pennsylvania

Grand Jury report had created within the US. I thought to myself, he has one of the most difficult jobs in the world. It takes a great deal of resilience to withstand the constant scrutiny he must be encountering with the revelations of sexual misconduct emerging in the news every day.

I understood the importance of the Commission's work and what it meant to the Church and to the survivors of abuse. I said a silent prayer: "Lord, bless these men and give them strength to persevere during the difficult times ahead."

We arrived at the airport and I made my flight with time to spare. Thankfully, the plane had WiFi, so I was able to work during the five hour flight home. I got out my notes and surfed the web, learning all I could about the organizations and people involved in the Pope's Commission. There was so much I had to learn. Little did I know that this was just beginning of my journey!

Acknowledgments

I MUST FIRST acknowledge that this work was inspired by God. I felt His presence throughout much of the writing process, and then He sent me two messengers along the way to give me encouragement. The messengers were complete strangers who knew nothing of what I was writing, or anything about me at all. Yet, they both told me I should not doubt myself; that this was a meaningful book, and I should not give up.

I also thank my brothers for always being there for me when I needed them. I hope this book helps ease in some small way the pain and suffering you have endured. I wrote this book for you, because I want you to know how much you are loved.

Next, I must thank several individuals who contributed significantly to this book.

I thank Rick Benzel, my publisher and editor, who made significant editorial contributions to this work; and Susan Shankin, who also read the manuscript and provided suggestions. It was an amazing experience working with you both and I am honored and humbled that you dropped everything to help me meet my deadline.

I thank James Cisneros for his contribution in helping me in the development of the screenplay, *A Letter to the Pope.*

I thank Kevin Barnard for his contributions to the design and production of this book—including the beautiful cover.

I sincerely thank Pastor Dan Smith, who was kind to me and generous with his time. He helped me on my spiritual journey. His wise advice led me to take another chance on love. He is a dedicated missionary, a brilliant scholar, and a wonderful human being.

I would like to thank Dr. Jonathan Fielding for serving as my mentor during my doctoral studies at UCLA, and for providing me with the foundation I needed to tackle this important public health issue.

I owe Gabe more than he will ever know. Thank you for being such a kind and caring soul.

About the Author

Jennifer Wortham, Dr.PH has served as a healthcare executive and consultant for over 30 years. She has worked with several world-class hospitals and health care delivery systems including the University of California, Los Angeles, Ashe Student Health Services, Kaiser Permanente, and Children's Hospital of Los Angeles, among others.

She graduated from UCLA with a master's and a doctorate in public health. She teaches graduate courses at the UCLA Fielding School of Public Health.

Dr. Wortham lectures internationally on the application of Lean, a management approach that helps healthcare organizations deliver greater value to patients based on lessons learned from Toyota. Dr. Wortham serves on the Board of Advisors for California State University, San Bernardino, and she was recently elected to serve on the board of the Desert Healthcare District.

In 2018, Jennifer founded the Solace Institute to promote peace and reconciliation for survivors of abuse.

Made in USA - Kendallville, IN
1179823_9780999580127